To my dearest N.,
I hope you enjoy reading my story!

From Aradippou to the Moon

Lots of love,
Eleftheria

From
Aradippou
to the
Moon

A memoir

ELLIE PATSALOS

Copyright © 2023 Ellie Patsalos

The moral right of the author has been asserted.

Apart from any fair dealing for the purposes of research or private study, or criticism or review, as permitted under the Copyright, Designs and Patents Act 1988, this publication may only be reproduced, stored or transmitted, in any form or by any means, with the prior permission in writing of the publishers, or in the case of reprographic reproduction in accordance with the terms of licences issued by the Copyright Licensing Agency. Enquiries concerning reproduction outside those terms should be sent to the publishers.

Patsalos Consulting
2 New Street Square,
London, EC4A 3BZ

ISBN 978 1 39993 871 6

British Library Cataloguing in Publication Data.
A catalogue record for this book is available from the British Library.

Printed and bound by CPI Group (UK) Ltd, Croydon, CR0 4YY
Typeset in 11pt Minion Pro by Troubador Publishing Ltd, Leicester, UK

*For my grandchildren Iris and Raphael,
and any future grandchildren.*

Contents

1	Walking on the Moon	1
2	Life in the Village	8
3	*Peripatos* (A Walk)	16
4	Leaving Home	22
5	Dancing at the Thanet	28
6	Christmas Eve at the Casino	34
7	A Village Wedding	39
8	Miss Ellie in America	44
9	Motherhood	52
10	Trees in the Swimming Pool	59
11	A Circle of Friends and Family	65
12	Finding My Feet	71
13	Treatment	78
14	The New Account	84
15	Mergers and Acquisitions	90
16	The Ellie Effect	97
17	New Business	105
18	On the Board	110
19	Maria and Nicolas	116
20	July 2005 (7/7)	123
21	The 7/7 Aftermath	131
22	Losing Eleni	138
23	Recognition	142

Contents

24	Changing Expectations	149
25	A Funeral, an Engagement and a Wedding	157
26	Six Retirement Parties	165
27	Skydiving	171
28	Climbing Mountains	178
29	Descent	185
30	Postcards from Antarctica	191
31	Exotic Travels	200
32	Iris	207
33	The Pandemic	211
34	Back to the Village	219
35	Epilogue: More than a Dream	226
Acknowledgements		231

Walking on the Moon

I remember the night the first men landed on the moon. I was walking in the village with my grandmother, and we were coming back from my aunt's house. It was 20th July 1969, and everybody was talking about the moon landing. I found it all so exciting, but my grandmother was convinced that it was impossible. She asked me if I believed it was happening, if it was real.

She said, 'Do you believe God will allow a man to walk on the moon?'

I said, 'Yes, *yiayia*, of course it's real. They wouldn't make it up!' But my grandmother was adamant; she would never believe it happened.

When you live in a small village, something like that seems incredible. That night, it struck me what a big thing it is to actually go to the moon, and that's something that has stayed with me until now. My fascination with space started that night in Cyprus when I was a teenager walking with my grandmother. I still think of travelling into space today, and with the latest developments in space travel I believe it is now a real possibility before I die.

I was born on 22nd May 1954, in a small village called Aradippou with a population of approximately five thousand people. We were a big family; my mother and father had seven children, and I was the fifth child and the youngest daughter.

Youla was the eldest daughter, followed by my brother Mitsios, then my other two sisters Miroula and Elli, then me and my other two brothers, Takis and Nikos, who was the youngest. My parents came from different backgrounds, but they were the same age and born in the same village. In those days, if you married someone from a different village to yours, they were called a '*xenos*', meaning foreigner, even if they were only from Larnaca, the closest town.

My mother was an intelligent woman, but she was not educated past primary-school level. My father only went to school for three years, and then he had to help his family in cultivating the fields or anywhere else they needed help. They married very young and, as was the custom then, neither had had a previous relationship. Both of my parents were very religious, and it was an arranged marriage. Although my mother had so many children, she liked to look after us herself and would make sure we were always beautifully dressed and groomed. She wore makeup when she went out to special events, and the seams of her stockings were always straight. My mother was a very serious person, whereas my father was more relaxed. He liked telling jokes and, as a younger man, participated in the various village plays performed during the festivals. In later years, he used to recite passages from those plays, which we loved to hear.

In some ways my mother was a typical housewife, but very private and not interested in gossip; for one thing, she didn't have the time! She was understandably always very busy, having to look after seven children, cooking, cleaning and washing everything by hand, in the days before washing machines were affordable. I remember all of her routines and errands, from getting water from the nearby communal fountain – I had to wait at the fountain when I was very young with my sister Elli, so that our mother wouldn't lose her turn in the queue – to baking enough fresh bread to last for a whole week, usually on a Wednesday. She also helped my dad, who was a merchant, and kept supplies at home. Customers would come to buy all kinds of things, including ladies' stockings, children's clothes and shoes, gifts for weddings, engagements and christenings, pots and pans, and everything that a household needed. Over the weekends when my father was working in the fields, or during the week when he was in Larnaca or Nicosia getting supplies, my mother would serve the customers and keep back a little money for herself. She liked having her own money in addition to the money she received for the daily household expenses, so she had the independence to spend that money as she wished. She was very particular about cleanliness and kept the house in top condition, a trait her daughters inherited from her. My mother was tough in her own way, and she controlled what was going on in the house, but my dad was the big decision-maker for all the important things in the household.

I come from a long line of dynamic women. My maternal grandmother was an amazing woman, and her family name, Teralli, was very well known in the village. She was the only daughter among seven brothers, so she grew up to be very tough. Her husband had two given names, Nicolas Eleftherios, and my name, Eleftheria, is derived from one of them. Eleftheria is a patriotic name which means freedom or liberty, and it is not very commonly used. The irony of having such a name was that, although my name meant freedom, I had no freedom whatsoever to make my own decisions for many years.

When I was born my sister Youla, the eldest child, was sent to ask my grandparents, 'What should we call the new baby?' I was my parents' fifth child, and they had already used my grandmother's name, Eleni, for my older sister Elli, so they wanted to call me after my grandfather. Since my grandfather had two names, my grandparents told my sister, 'You can choose whether it's Nicki – from Nicolas – or Eleftheria, from Eleftherios.' As Youla walked back to our house, she weighed up the two names and decided that Eleftheria was more unusual. So, in the end, my sister was the one who chose my name.

It is very much expected that you give your parents' names to your children, and by the time I had children my parents already had nine grandchildren, as my sisters married earlier than me. We felt that if the first one was a boy, we would call him Nicolas after my father-in-law, and if it was a girl, we would call her Xenia – after my dad's name, Xenophon. There were no other Xenias in the family; all the girls were called after my mum, whose name was Anastasia, but because our daughter came first, we had to call her Maria after Philip's mother, since this was their first grandchild! Later, when my son Nicolas was born, he was the only Nicolas Patsalos because my husband Philip was an only child, and none of his father's side had any children, so Nicolas was the bearer of the Patsalos name and therefore had to be named after his grandfather. My parents were happy with our decision because they already had so many grandchildren bearing their name, but I really liked the name Xenia. Looking back, we should have given it to Maria as her middle name. My sister's choice of first name for me also meant that my initials were EXP – Eleftheria Xenophon Patsalos – which sounded like 'EXP'. Later when I became a partner, the *UK Accountancy Journal* gently made fun of my initials, saying that of course it was appropriate because I specialised in working with expats!

My sister's name, Youla, is derived from the name Kyriakoulla, and she was named after our great-uncle, my maternal grandmother's brother, who was named Kyriakos. From a very young age, Kyriakos was blind, but he was a remarkable man and achieved so much for someone who couldn't see. Because my mother had the house next to my grandmother and Kyriakos was so helpful to her with the children, she named my sister, her first child, after him. He loved working in his vegetable garden, which he tended lovingly every day. He cultivated all kinds of vegetables, which my mother and grandmother used in their cooking. He also loved telling us stories. When we were very young, we'd go to see him and say, '*Pappou, Pappou* (Grandad), tell us a story from your mind.' He made up all his stories because he'd never read anything. I understand from my grandmother that he remembered seeing things and lost his sight at the age of four or five, but he had an amazing imagination, in the way that people who lose one of their five senses cultivate other senses to compensate. *Pappou* Kyriakos would come up with amazing stories for all the young kids, not only my sisters and me but all the kids in the neighbourhood, and my cousins heard his stories too. Occasionally he would repeat stories, but most of them were new, and every time he told us one, we were mesmerised. He could have been an author, and later, when we were older, someone came to the village and wrote all his stories down in a book.

My maternal grandfather Nicolas was a butcher, as were all the men in his family. My uncles, my mother's brothers, became butchers too, which was seen as a more prestigious job than working in the fields. Two of the brothers, Andreas and Loizos, emigrated to Australia when they were young men in order to find a better life. One of their uncles who was already there supported them, so they managed to get the appropriate visas. My mother's sister Chryssi and her brother Charalambos emigrated to the UK with their families, also for a better economic future, so in Cyprus my mother had her older sister Stavroula and two brothers, Markos and Kostas.

I was very young when my grandfather died, but I remember the funeral; it was a very big funeral, everyone dressed in black and crying. It was the first funeral I attended, and it made a big impression on me. In those days, after your husband died, it was traditional to wear black, and so I remember my grandmother wearing black clothes and a black shawl all her life. She lived in a small house next to ours with four rooms, and one of the rooms was later converted into a bedroom where my older brother, my sisters and I slept.

My paternal grandfather was called Demetris, and he was a handsome man, very tall and with a wicked sense of humour. My father took after him! I remember him wearing the traditional black *vraka*, a type of men's trousers, that were the customary attire for men during those years. He, like my dad, was involved in buying and selling goods. In particular, he used to buy handmade lace tablecloths and decorative pieces from his suppliers in the iconic village of Lefkara in the Larnaca district of Cyprus and sell them to his customers. Lefkara, by coincidence, is my husband Philip's home village, where he and his parents were born! My brother Mitsios is named after my grandfather (Mitsios is the derivative of Demetris).

My paternal grandmother, Myrofora, died of cancer before I was born. My dad told me that she was a quiet woman and a devoted housewife and mother. My sister Miroula is named after her. The death of my grandmother meant that my dad and all his siblings grew up with only their dad to look after them.

My dad had five siblings. The oldest sister, Maria, emigrated to Australia with her husband when their children were very young to find a better future. His oldest brother Andreas died relatively young, struck by lightning during a bad thunderstorm. He had a younger brother, Avraam, and two younger sisters, Elli and Georgina. My aunt Georgina married Louis Michael, who lived in England, and followed him to London after they were married. Later, they moved to Margate and owned restaurants, where I would work during my student years in the UK.

As my older sisters grew up, sometimes they had platonic likings for the local boys; only looking, not even speaking. When she was a teenager, my oldest sister Youla liked somebody that way. The boy lived opposite my aunt's house, so she went over there a lot. They wouldn't even talk, but eventually my mother got wind of it and told Youla to stop going to my aunt's house on her own. After that, when she wanted to go to my aunt's house, she had to be chaperoned by someone else.

When Youla got engaged, she was only sixteen. She was nine years older than me, and she was acting in a play, wearing a beautiful Grecian costume – I still have a photograph of what she was wearing that day. Savvas, her husband, saw her and fell in love with her. Savvas was a teacher, and his family was poor, but he was very clever and managed to finish his studies. At that time, in the early sixties, being a teacher was a great achievement since it was very difficult to get into the Teachers' Training Academy. The way matchmaking happened in those days was that the man who wanted to ask for a woman's hand in marriage sent a close family member to express his interest, so a friend of the family asked my father to go to his sister's house to discuss the proposal. My mother told him before he left our house, 'You go and tell them we don't have a daughter old enough to be engaged.' However, a few hours later, he returned home and said, 'Our daughter is now engaged!' My mother was furious, not because she didn't approve of Savvas but because she felt that Youla was too young. In the end, my sister had a very happy life with Savvas, since he was cultivated and took good care of her, but at the time she was quite perplexed and was more interested in playing hopscotch with her girlfriends. She said to our mother, 'Who is this man, and why is he coming to our house every day?' Young girls were very naïve in those days, but that sort of thing happened a lot.

Life in the Village

Like most people in our village, my parents had land that they cultivated, with olive, carob and fig trees. We had to gather them depending on the season, picking figs or carobs in the summer and harvesting olives in the autumn.

Although he worked in the fields for his entire life, my father was mostly an entrepreneur, buying and selling things. He started off small; he would go around the village on his bicycle selling thread to make cloth, which was called *nema*. Gradually, he replaced the bicycle with a car and started buying and selling women's, men's and children's clothes, including underwear, socks, school uniforms, trousers, shirts and shoes. Later, he moved into selling household goods for local girls who were getting married and had to have a dowry with all the necessary things for a new household. My brother Mitsios joined my father's business after elementary school and was appointed to the second business venture. Mitsios never liked this job and always complained that my dad didn't send him to secondary school, like all his friends.

From very early on, my father and I worked closely together as a team, much more than any of my other siblings. I had a very active involvement in the business from a young age. Unlike my three older sisters and older brother, I was immediately drawn into my father's work. He would take me with him to Nicosia and Larnaca, to buy goods from his suppliers. I became quite a whiz kid because I was very good at maths, so they kept asking me to solve complicated questions! I believe the reason I was so relentless in my client service delivery in my career is because my father trained me from a very young age. All our customers were women, and women are very demanding; they were also the ones who held the purse strings! When they asked us for things we didn't have, we would say, 'OK, we have that in stock, and I will deliver it by bicycle,' even if we didn't and I actually had to go to Larnaca to get it. The most important thing was to keep the customers happy. I realised then how much I loved being in this client service environment, which was something that would stay with me and shape the rest of my working life.

I always loved hard work in general. During my early days in elementary school, everybody in the household had to do chores; one had to contribute to the family, and I was one of the most energetic members. Because I was primarily more business-minded, I didn't really do a lot of housework; my older sisters helped with that, but I did a lot of other things to help my parents. Sometimes when they were buying the clothes and sheets for their daughters' dowries, my father's customers would pay him in woven baskets that he would then sell on to parts of Cyprus where they were growing citrus fruit – oranges, grapefruits, tangerines and lemons – to be exported to the UK and other countries. To be sturdy enough to hold the fruit, the baskets had to be reinforced by weaving thin pieces of steel through them, and after school, when we had finished our homework, we would do at least ten of these baskets each.

I was a very good student in elementary school. One of our classmates, who was not very bright, needed help, and having an entrepreneurial mindset, I thought I could benefit from this and make some money or get some goodies in exchange for helping her with maths and other subjects she struggled with. I would tell her, 'You can copy my maths,' or whatever it was, 'but in exchange, you can either give me some of your pocket money or some of the lovely things your grandfather sells in his shop.' I would get chocolates, pencils with little rubbers, sharpeners, pencil cases, nice writing paper and other goodies.

There wasn't much entertainment in the neighbourhood before TV came to the village, only the radio. In the evenings, the women would either sit outside or between each other's houses and talk about what was going on in the village, gossiping about this and that and analysing it all, while the children played around them. The boys would play hide-and-seek or run around a small stream together, and because I was a real tomboy I would always go and play with them. We had long, long summers, with lots of mischief because we were bored. I was always the leader of the gang, in charge of all the mischief; I had that leadership quality, and all my friends would rally behind me.

When I was a teenager, we didn't have summer holidays as such, but because my dad had the car he used for business, every summer he would take it for its annual MOT, so we emptied the whole car, climbed in and drove to the mountains. There were no hotels, or none that we could have afforded to stay in as they were a real luxury in those days, so we would stay in monasteries. We would go there on a pilgrimage with our pots and pans, sometimes just us and sometimes with another family. It wasn't much of a luxurious holiday, but it was much cooler in the mountains and still a break from the heat we'd had all summer.

There was a cinema in the village, but we didn't have much pocket money, just half a shilling to get into the cinema, and we used whatever was left to buy sweets or chocolate. On Sunday, after church and lunch, the climax of our day was to go to the afternoon matinee to see two films, usually Westerns or sometimes a Steve Reeves movie. We would stand outside the cinema for as long as we could, hoping an older brother or cousin would come along and pay for our tickets so we could use all of our pocket money to buy sweets. Also, if the second film was X-rated, we knew we weren't allowed to stay and watch it, so a few of us would sometimes go to the toilets during the break and then come back out when it was dark. Eventually the manager realised what we were doing and threw us out!

We were a very Orthodox Christian society and going to church was very important. During elementary school we were expected to wear our school uniform and go to church with our teacher. During Holy Week, Easter being the most important celebration in the church calendar, we would go to church every afternoon. I was a member of the local choir, and on Good Friday we practised and sang a key hymn from the Bible, *Ai Geneai Pasai*. After the main ceremony in church, the Epitaphios, a wooden structure with the body of Christ and lots of flowers around it, was taken out in a procession around the village. We loved this.

One of the things we also loved about Easter was that it was customary to wear new clothes. There wasn't much to do in the village, and most of the time I was helping my dad with his deliveries, so Sundays and public and religious holidays were an excuse for us to go out and be seen, wear new clothes and see the boys we secretly liked. Christmas didn't matter so much when it came to clothes, but Easter was at springtime, the weather was getting warmer and everyone wanted to be wearing something new. Over the Easter weekend, you would go to church in the morning and evening on Holy Saturday when the *Christos Anesti* took place. After the ceremony of Christ rising from the dead, the boys would throw firecrackers. The other tradition was that every neighbourhood would put a heap of wood together and light it, as though they were killing Judas Iscariot – just like they do in the UK with Guy Fawkes.

During Holy Week and Christmas, everyone fasted. The children only had to fast during Holy Week. Before we went to Holy Communion, we weren't supposed to eat or drink anything. Once my younger brothers got into trouble because there was a lady near our house who sold sweets, and they bought sweets before Holy Communion. A few years later I did a similarly naughty thing with my cousin Maria, my aunt Stavroula's daughter. During Easter, all the housewives, including my mother and aunt, would bake special cookies to eat on Easter Sunday and beyond. One Easter I went over to my cousin's house to help on Good Friday. My aunt Stavroula had just freshly baked all these goodies, and Maria and I had to take them from the back of the house to the kitchen in the front. On the way, we each ate one of the cookies, even though we were expected to take Communion in the morning on Holy Saturday. We knew that what we were doing was wrong, but we couldn't resist them, they smelled so good and tasted fantastic. So really, we did what my brothers had done – we just never told anybody and were not found out!

I finished elementary school when I was eleven years old, and my plan was to go to the Greek high school in Larnaca since all my friends were going there. However, my father told me that I had to go to the American Academy in Larnaca to learn English, which he called 'the language of the future'. He wanted me to go to private school, even though it was very expensive and the public schools were free. It felt strange being away from my friends from elementary school, but I quickly made new ones, whom I am still in touch with. There were four of us from Aradippou in my year: me, my cousin Antonis, another boy named George and Liana, a girl who I did not know very well at first, but we became very close friends. At the American Academy we had the whole weekend off, and the students at the Greek school were envious because they only got Sundays off – but I was actually envious of them, because I loved school so much that I would have happily gone on Saturdays too, and I was rather sad that I was never given the option.

It was strange at first, attending a mixed-gender school, though later all high schools in Cyprus became mixed-gender. In addition to having boys in our classes, the main change for all of us was that the official language at the school was English, and this was very strictly enforced. No Greek was allowed, and if during the day a prefect caught anyone speaking Greek, that student would be given a 'ticket'. The holder of the 'ticket' would try his or her best to trick another pupil to speak Greek and thus pass it on. Whoever was still holding the 'ticket' by the end of the day would have points deducted from their average grade for that semester, so this was a big deal.

During the first three years, and before we were split into University Section or Commercial Section, we were the junior students, so the older girls would boss us around a lot. The youngest students were easy to trick into speaking Greek so they often ended up with the 'ticket', but later, as we became more senior, we would follow the same tactics and find easy victims!

I still remember a few milestones and events, for example the annual games that the American Academy participated in with the English School, the other renowned school in Cyprus, which was an English-speaking school based in Nicosia. Both schools to this day continue to be the top schools in the whole island. Before each encounter, the head of PT (Physical Training) would get on stage after the morning service at the school Assembly Theatre and encourage us to be very vocal in supporting our athletes during the games. It was so uplifting to hear the whole school singing the teams' songs at the tops of our voices! In the third form, when I was fourteen, I was allowed by my parents to go to the English School to attend the various games, and we were always impressed by how much more fashionable the English School girls were. During PT classes, I was always selected for the running team or long jump team, but since I wasn't allowed to attend practice in the afternoons, I never made it onto the school teams. One of my favourite hobbies was dancing; I loved learning the Greek and Cypriot folk dances. I would spend my afternoons with my friends from the Greek school, learning the dances for our national celebrations on 25th March and 1st April. We were not taught these dances at the American Academy I attended, but I didn't want to miss out.

Another memorable practice at the American Academy was the celebration of Thanksgiving every November. We were asked to bring foodstuffs to school and visited poor families in Larnaca with our teachers. This was a very valuable experience and taught us at an early age that there were families who were not as privileged as us. Later in my life I would attend Thanksgiving dinners in America, and this turned out to be a good preparation for that too. Also, before I attended the American Academy I never knew about Valentine's Day and why it was celebrated, but sadly I never attended the Annual Balls organised by the school because no one could take me to Larnaca in the evenings and none of my sisters could drive.

Our school was linked to an evangelical Christian church in America, so we had several young male teachers posted to the American Academy for a few years' secondment. Needless to say, they were all very handsome and all the single female teachers and quite a few of the students were in love with them!

One summer I was allowed to go camping with the school at the Troodos Mountains, where the American Academy had a campsite. I was so thrilled to be allowed to go with my friends, Liana, Koula and the others. We slept in tents separately from the boys and everyone had chores to do each day, but we also went on long walks in the mountain trails, had group exercises and read the Bible frequently. At night, after dinner, we sat around the campfire and sang songs and hymns. It was a magical experience. At the end of the trip, I returned home and declared that I was a born-again Christian, but I admit that my new calling didn't last very long. The whole family was bemused by my decision, and they were not very surprised when I got over it!

Christmas was also a very special time because in the week before we finished the semester for the holidays, we had a celebration and sang all the beautiful Christmas carols. Later in life, I continued to attend Christmas carol services in London when my children were at school, and later when my firm organised them at a church in the City close to our offices. No matter how busy I was, I never missed them.

Sometimes I miss that simple life, but I know that even if I were to go back, Cyprus isn't that simple now; even Aradippou isn't the same. I still like the quiet pace of life, and sometimes I feel nostalgic and miss the way things were, but even if you live on a beautiful island, it can still be boring if you are there twenty-four hours a day.

Peripatos (A Walk)

As we grew older, it was customary for people in our village to go for a walk – the *peripatos* – on Sunday afternoons. We would go down the road from Aradippou towards Larnaca, the next town, where my school was. We were not allowed to sit or have a drink at the two cafés on the way until we were older, but from the age of thirteen to sixteen, we girls could go for a walk and the boys would walk behind us. They were not allowed to talk to us, but we could hear them talk among themselves about us. The fact that they were behind us was still a big deal, and we would wear our very best clothes and shoes. The purpose of the walk was really to show off our clothes, and there was always a lot of preparation and agonising about what clothes to wear because we always wanted to wear something different. As the youngest daughter in the family, I always fought with my sister Elli, who used to wear my nice shoes as if they were casual and didn't even try to hide that she was doing it! I kept my shoes very clean in their box because we only had one pair for winter and a couple of pairs of sandals for the summer, unlike now when young girls have so many clothes and shoes. We would usually wear skirts and jumpers, but I remember when I was sixteen years old and for the first time, I was allowed a long-sleeved winter dress; I can still recall its colour and texture.

Outside national and religious holidays, the *peripatos* was where everybody congregated on Sunday afternoons. That was the excitement of the Sunday; everyone would look forward to it, and even when we went to the mountains in the summer months to babysit, we always wanted to return in time for the *peripatos*. Older girls like my sisters could sit in the café on their own, but not with boys unless they were their brothers or first cousins. They would sit and have soft drinks and sweets, like *loukoumades*, which were round fried pastries full of honey and syrup.

There was a lot of pressure for girls to behave decently and avoid getting a bad reputation. We weren't allowed to wear trousers for a long time; I think it was just before I came to England in the summer of 1972, when I was about seventeen, that I was allowed to wear trousers. In the towns it was different, but where we grew up, it wasn't seen as proper. We would sometimes go to the beach with my sister Youla, her husband Savvas and their children Eleni, Xenakis and Eleftheria, but girls were not supposed to show their legs, so we didn't learn to swim. If I ever wore a bathing suit, it was borrowed from a friend of mine, and they would have got that bathing suit from someone in the town. It seems crazy to think about it now, but that's how it was. In our back yard, there was a big well, and my mother would say to me, 'If you do something to disgrace our family, I will fall into that well and die.' She repeated that the day I left for Cyprus in 1972. Good behaviour, particularly with boys, was entrenched in us. Of course, that was not the case for everyone. Some girls didn't really care, or their parents did not have that sort of deep, old-fashioned thinking, and it was different in our village than in the towns. You could not disgrace your family because if you had a bad reputation, you could not marry well.

My husband Philip laughed when he found this out, but in the village, being engaged was viewed in exactly the same way as being married, so you were allowed to have sex when you were engaged. On the day of the engagement there was a proper ceremony, when the priest blessed the new couple, and it was like a miniature wedding. Engagements always led to marriage, and nobody got divorced. If you had broken it off with someone, how could you walk past them on the street? It didn't mean that you didn't crave the feeling of holding somebody's hand in springtime or going to the movies with a boy. It was a natural thing. No wonder young women rebel when they are brought up like that. Of course, things have changed now, even back home; young people now have relationships just like everywhere else.

When we were teenagers in high school, Youla and Savvas, his sister Chrystalla and her husband Theodoros Sideras, who were also teachers, would rent a house up in Pedoulas, a small village in the Troodos Mountains, for the summer. Because we all lived near the sea, and it was so hot during the summer months, many families came there from all over Cyprus to get some relief from the summer heat. This was a luxury that not everyone could afford, but being teachers, they had a good income. They would go to Pedoulas at the end of June, when the schools closed, and then return at the end of August to prepare their lessons and administrative chores to be ready for the opening of their schools at the beginning of September. We loved going to Pedoulas to visit them.

At the time, my sisters Miroula and Elli and I were living at home. Youla was the only one of us who was married, but the rest of us would take it in turns to spend a week or so visiting them in Pedoulas. Periodically Savvas would return to Aradippou from the mountain to take care of certain matters and take one or two of us girls back with him. I would often go with my best friend Maro, who was the same age as me, and the niece of Savvas and Chrystalla. Each couple had two children, and Maro and I acted as babysitters for them. I remember that we had some great times looking after the children over the years, including my beautiful niece Eleni when she was a young girl.

At Pedoulas and all over the mountain there were beautiful little churches, and we'd go to visit them early in the morning.

After breakfast, in mid-morning, we would go to the local café, which was called *Vrysi* (meaning 'fountain') and play cards, have a drink and pass the time until we had to go home for lunch and a siesta. In the evenings we'd go out for dinner or for long walks and sit in one of the many cafés to have drinks and eat local delicacies. One summer, we met two boys from Nicosia in the café. We used to take Eleni for walks and the two boys would follow us and speak to us, although we didn't respond much; we only told them our names. At night, they started visiting our neighbourhood and sang lovely songs near our house. Youla and Savvas were wondering who they were and why they came every night. They had no clue that the boys were coming for Maro and me!

My sisters and I were ardent readers. Now I work with a charity that supports financially disadvantaged children to go to university, and I get so excited when I meet young people who tell me that they love reading. I know it will help them to escape their present environment and dream about the future. Books bring so much enjoyment into your life; they help your imagination run wild. I remember being their age and going to university, and how important reading was to me. Two of my three brothers-in-law were headmasters, so they had libraries full of books. In those long summers, I would read all the time, everything from detective stories to Dostoyevsky. I read *War and Peace,* and *Les Misérables* by Victor Hugo. Years later when I saw the show in London I thought, 'I know this story!' My older brother Mitsios once brought home *Lady Chatterley's Lover*, a very scandalous book in those days. My oldest sister wasn't at our family home then because she was married, but Miroula and Elli were still at home. We took it in turns to read the book, and we were very careful to put it back in exactly the same place so that Mitsios wouldn't realise we were reading it! My family didn't have a TV, so sometimes we used to go to a neighbour's house to watch our favourite shows like *The Fugitive, Dr Kildare* and *Flipper.*

As I grew older, my dad would trust me to go from Aradippou to Nicosia or Larnaca by taxi to buy the stock we wanted. When I went into Nicosia, I would always choose the things that I liked, and I would get all this funky stuff and bring it to the village. There were white tights with all sorts of different designs, which were popular in the sixties; some had straight lines sewn across them and some had flowers. I would come home wearing the best ones, which became fashion items; all my friends and the girls in the village wanted them too.

I remember one evening I overheard my dad telling my mum in Greek, 'Our daughter, Eleftheria, is so amazing. She helps me so much; she really gets it.' I was so proud to hear my dad say this, because I really looked up to my parents. I remember the feeling of getting back from a hard day's work in the summer, and my mother would bring my favourite food, and I felt so content that I had worked hard that day to earn my dinner.

As well as being entrepreneurially minded, like my father, I was always a good student academically and in the top five in our class in the Commercial Section. The other students were Meropi, Chrystalla, Koula and Liana – all girls, you'll notice, and not a single boy! One year before my scheduled graduation from the American Academy, I realised that there was no point in staying for my seventh and final year because girls weren't allowed to do A-levels. The boys could choose Physics, Economics and other subjects that they needed to get into university, but the girls were only allowed to take O-levels (now known as GCSEs). Thus, there was no way I was going to be part of the University Section but only the Commercial Section. It was expected that once a girl finished the Commercial Section, she would get a job as a secretary, but I was quite firm that I did not want to get a job, get married and have a child by the time I was nineteen. My sister Miroula did exactly that, she married her husband Andreas, and although she finished high school and did another business course for a year, she wasn't allowed to work. My sister Elli didn't go to high school and was married at eighteen to Savakis.

Because our school did not teach A-levels to girls, I decided that the only way to do it was to study in London. Therefore, with a sad heart, I left all my friends and classmates in the summer of 1972 to go to London. I didn't see most of them for ten years, when we had our tenth-anniversary reunion in Larnaca. It was so exciting to see them there, especially as most of them made the effort to attend. Getting to England was not straightforward, however, and it would take me on a very different path to the ones my sisters followed. Even before I spoke to my father, I knew I had a battle ahead of me.

Leaving Home

In the summer of 1971, when I was seventeen years old, my cousin Kyriakos, who lived in London, visited Cyprus for a holiday with his friends. At the time he was attending the Teachers' Training College and we had long conversations about what it was like to study in London, and I became even more excited at the prospect of going to England to study. In Aradippou, girls were not allowed to go to university, but my cousin put the grains of these expectations in my mind. No matter how much I talked about it, my father was relentless. He kept saying, 'No, no, you can't go to England. You must stay, get a job and get married.' Women were under pressure to stay close to their families and marry someone in the village.

My mother didn't want me to go to England either, but I knew she would go with whatever my father decided. My father even recited an old poem to me that said women should not leave home, 'because the wolf will eat them'. The more he talked like that, the more I cried. I told him I would stop eating; I would go on a hunger strike and die. I even tried to get my father's suppliers in Nicosia and Larnaca to help me persuade him. My brothers-in-law, Savvas and Andreas, who were teachers, told my father, 'She's clever, and it would be a shame not to let her go.'

Then, coincidentally, Kyriakos' older sister Ellou came to Cyprus for a month's holiday in July 1972. I told her that I wanted to go to university in England, and she said, 'You must come and stay with us. We have plenty of space.' She spoke to my father, who said no at first, but everyone tried their hardest to persuade him that he should allow me to study in London. If he had put his foot down and said, 'No, you are not going anywhere because you are a girl, and you are my daughter, and I make the final decision,' that would have been it. My life would have been totally different.

There were three key moments in my life. The first was when my father asked me to go to Nicosia to get a passport. I knew that if I got a passport, I would be allowed to go to England to study – and that's exactly what happened. On the first of August 1972 I boarded a plane with my cousin Ellou and her daughter Mary, heading for London. I will discuss the other two key moments later on.

When I arrived in England, I was only eighteen and very scared. It was the first time I had ever been on a plane, and I had never left my home country before. I was living in a strange house with Ellou, my cousin whom I had only met once, so the blood relationship was there, but we had no other kind of relationship initially. Ellou's husband Stavros welcomed me to their home as his oldest daughter. He was very proud of me, and he and Ellou asked me to mentor their children, in particular Mary, their oldest child. Mary was going through a difficult time as a teenager. Then there were the twin boys, Chrisos and George, as well as the youngest daughter, Eleftheria. At that age, I had a sort of instinctive confidence, but I was very naïve. I wasn't sure about myself, even though I was strong enough to live away from my family, concentrate on my studies while living in my cousin's house in London and persevere with my dreams. My determination and my strict focus on what I wanted to achieve enabled me to overcome these obstacles.

Above all, I worked very hard because I did not want to let my parents down. They had sacrificed a lot economically for me to come to England, because even though my father's business was doing quite well, he had to sell a couple of pieces of land to fund my education because there was no spare cash around to pay for it. However, it all balanced out, because that was part of my inheritance. My father built my three sisters a house each on a piece of land, and he sold two pieces of land for me.

At first, all the London houses looked exactly the same to me. There was a little shrub outside my cousin's house, and that's how I used to tell it apart from the others. When the shrub perished, I went back to not knowing which one was which! Shortly after I arrived in London, I realised that there were a lot of things I didn't know. Because my cousin was working, and she had four children, I had to learn how to cook. In Cyprus I had helped my mother with various household tasks, but I wasn't very involved in the kitchen, so back then I didn't know how to boil an egg! Every day I waited until my cousin went out to work and then I called my aunt, Thea Vasoula, who was married to my uncle Charalambos; they lived in London and she worked from home. I would say, 'Thea, I need to cook beans today. How do I cook them?' She explained everything I needed to do, starting with, 'Well, put the beans in the water...' I gradually learned to cook, do the housework and clean the whole house on weekends. Now I love to entertain, and later on in London I organised lavish parties, even while I was working. I love the social aspect of entertaining but would be the first to admit that I am still not the best cook. Over the years, there are a few dishes that I have learned to do well, but I would always rather be working or running than cooking.

It was hard to acclimatise to the weather, which was so rainy and grey, and to adjust to London after living in a small village. I missed my family terribly and would cry all the time – it was tough, and although I had a strong personality, I was homesick. Also, I had an *amour*, Chris, whom I had left back home, so even though I had hardly seen him, I still missed him. A year later, he also came to London to study, but we still couldn't meet. Ellou said, 'My God, if your father found out you were seeing somebody, he would be very upset with us. We are responsible for looking after you.' My uncle Charalambos was very strict and old-fashioned, so I was scared to do anything in case he found out.

The following story – a funny and frustrating incident – illustrates just how old-fashioned Uncle Charalambos was. After I arrived in London, my parents finally decided to come and visit me. This was also the first time that they had been outside Cyprus, and after that my father got the travel bug and would travel outside Cyprus at least once a year. When they visited that first time, they stayed with Uncle Charalambos. I saw them almost every day and during one of our discussions, I told my father that I was going to see a movie with my cousin Neofytos – Aunt Stavroula's son, Maria's brother. He didn't say anything, since he knew Neofytos very well and trusted him fully. After a few minutes he called me back and told me that I wasn't allowed to go to the movies with my cousin because, according to Uncle Charalambos, if I was seen out with him, people wouldn't know he was my cousin, and they would think I was with my boyfriend. I was speechless at first, but then I got angry and I told my father that this was totally ridiculous and unacceptable. I had only told him I was going because he happened to be in London, and if he had not been, I would have gone with my cousin anyway. In the end I went to the cinema with Neofytos, and my father agreed with me, although my uncle was not happy. I was so glad that I wasn't staying with my uncle because I knew I would have had a difficult time.

Because I arrived in London in early August, it was too late to apply for a place at college. However, I managed to find a college in Whitechapel, in East London, through Neofytos, who did his A-levels there. At that time, Whitechapel wasn't a nice place, especially in the evenings with many drunken men hanging around. At first, I was scared of the Nigerians in my class, because

I had never seen anyone who looked like that in real life before, only in films. It was naïve, I know that now, and after a while, we all interacted with each other and became friends. Initially I found it quite difficult in class because the pronunciation was different from the accent we were used to from the American Academy with its American teachers, whereas the teachers in Whitechapel spoke so fast I couldn't understand anything. I found that the American teachers tended to speak more clearly, whereas the English swallowed most of their words, like I suppose I do now!

If I had stayed at the American Academy, I would have done the English O-level in my seventh year. I already had LCCs, qualifications from the London Chamber of Commerce, with distinctions in Maths, Commerce and English. I also had a number of other O-levels in History, Religious Knowledge, Maths and other subjects. At college, I did three A-levels and one O-level in one year. Our year, the class of 1972 to 1973, was the last to offer a one-year course for three A-levels; after that, it was extended to two years. I was working twenty-four hours a day to get all of the exams done satisfactorily! I studied Economics, British Constitution and Greek at A-level, and an O-level in English Language. I didn't study that much for the Greek A-level. I just read the books we were told to and wrote what I knew, and I got a C, though it turned out I didn't need it after all. I loved the Economics A-level, but British Constitution was very hard because I was unaware of the history or the politics of Britain.

One of the worst experiences I went through at the time was with my headteacher, who had to sign my University and College Admissions Service (UCAS) form. He thought I should only apply to polytechnics, which were considered to be in a second league to universities.

I said, 'No, I don't want to apply to polytechnics. I want to go to university, and only to the LSE (the London School of Economics)!'

He laughed at me and said, 'There's no way you can get into the LSE.' That made me even more determined to prove him wrong, which of course I did, but I knew I had to keep calm and avoid escalating the issue. I said I wanted to go because my cousin Neofytos was there and having visited it a number of times I realised that the LSE was the best place to study Economics, which I was planning to read. In the end, I compromised, and I put the LSE down as my third preference, a polytechnic as number one and Canterbury University as number two. The reason I chose Canterbury was that my aunt Georgina, my father's youngest sister, lived in Margate, so if I got admitted to Canterbury I could live in Margate and commute to university. My parents were adamant that I could not stay alone if I were to attend university outside London.

I was delighted when I got my grade offer from the LSE – two Bs, which was considered substantive in those days, unlike now when everyone is expected to get four As. In those days, apart from the students studying Maths or Econometrics, everyone else was getting Bs or lower. I was quite determined that if I got an offer from the LSE, I would work day and night to make it there. When my results came in, I got two Bs and a C at A-level, and my O-level in English Language, so I was very, very happy! This was the second out of the three key moments in my life. I knew that if I managed to get an Economics degree from the LSE, my professional career was guaranteed!

Dancing at the Thanet

Although my cousin Ellou and her family had a responsibility to keep an eye on me for my parents, I had so much fun at the LSE. I made a new best friend, Egly Hadjicharalambous, on our first day in the ladies' toilets. She came in, wearing a long dress, with light brown hair up in a bun and a very Bohemian look about her. We looked at each other, and I thought, 'Who is this interesting girl?' We started talking, and I realised she was from the English School in Nicosia, so immediately we had lots of things to talk about. We went for coffee at the university refectory and became the best of friends from that day on. We are still best friends, even though she now lives in Cyprus.

In her second year, Egly moved out of the house where she was staying with a Cypriot family that her parents knew and stayed in a Catholic home run by nuns in Notting Hill. Some nights I would go and stay there with her. We didn't have boyfriends, but sometimes I would tell white lies to Ellou so I could do other things. For example, I would say, 'Oh, there's an Economics professor from America coming to speak to us, so it will be too late to come home afterwards. Can I stay with Egly?' In the evenings when I stayed the night at Egly's room, the two of us would go to the Royal Albert Hall, or to the opera – we bought student tickets, right at the top of the venue, which were very cheap – and then we would go to dinner afterwards. We used to buy Dunhill International cigarettes, a very expensive brand in red and gold packets, though neither of us even knew how to smoke! We would light the cigarettes and sit just puffing away and not properly inhaling! Very silly, but that's the sort of thing you do when you're young. Egly would also visit me and stay with us at weekends, so both Ellou and Stavros got to know her very well and realised that she was a sensible girl like me.

Egly loved opera and classical music, and she introduced me to them as I had never really been exposed to such things before. She had, and still has, a wonderful ear for music; if she hears a song, she writes down the notes and plays it. Egly's mother was a teacher, her father was also a teacher and a classical musician, and her younger brother, Harris, was also very musical. She could play the concertos that she had learned for her music exams which she had passed in Cyprus. We would often go to the Shaw Library on the seventh floor of the LSE, book the music room, and sing and dance there. I would teach Egly Greek dances, which she had never been particularly interested in before, because she was too busy playing the piano and passing exams. I also taught her everything I knew about fashion, which has been my passion since those days. We both practised a dance called the *Hasapiko* and loved dancing it during social gatherings or when we had university outings and weekend retreats. Our favourite song to dance to was called *Frangosyriani*, and we were a good team. When we visited other Cypriot friends' houses, we always put Greek music on, and sang and danced the night away!

By that time, Chris, my *amour* from home, had arrived in London to go to university. He had completed his two-year military service as an officer and got his A-levels, so he was two years behind me academically. I would see him at parties sometimes with his non-Cypriot girlfriends. I was often upset when I saw them together, even though I knew that I could never be his girlfriend, since it wasn't allowed until we were engaged or married. Back then, there were no mobile phones which would have allowed us to call or communicate easily. In the evenings, Egly and I would listen to music and talk about boys we liked. Our conversations were always very sentimental – we would talk about these boys for hours, but we would never follow up any actions that we discussed. Between us, we never had any real relationships. One of the American students, who was visiting from Chicago, had a crush on me and kept asking me to go out with him on a date. I kept telling him that I couldn't, without explaining why. After many such discussions, I decided to tell him the reason – that in our culture dating was not seen as the right thing to do. He looked at me in such a horrified way – he was speechless! I decided that I would never say that to anyone else, even though it was true. I just pretended that I was in another relationship, which was much easier all round.

Not everyone felt the same way about relationships as they did back in my village. Egly's parents were from Nicosia, and they would very much have liked for her to go out with a boy, but she was very shy, so I would tell her, 'You should encourage me to become more modern, rather than me encouraging you to be more like me!'

Every summer, I would go back to Cyprus for four weeks. I only went back once at Christmas to attend my cousin Maria's engagement party to Vangelis. My aunt Georgina and my uncle Louis's family in Margate had a casino and two restaurants. Their three sons, Tony, Andrew and Theo, in descending age, were very young then but they all welcomed me. In the 1970s, Margate was very busy and flourishing. Many European students would come in the summer to take English courses. Also, at that time, holidaying abroad was not very common and few people could afford the cost, so English people would go to seaside resorts like Brighton, Blackpool, Ramsgate and Margate. I used to work at my aunt's restaurants for a few weeks after the exams finished and before I went to Cyprus in the summer to earn some pocket money. One of the restaurants, the Thanet, catered for well-to-do customers (the name Thanet was taken from the name of the local government district in Kent). That's where I learnt to set the table and make Irish coffees and various alcoholic drinks since I worked behind the bar some evenings. I also worked in the steam room and helped my aunt Georgina prepare the desserts – ice-cream sundaes and Peach Melba, which were always popular. Some Saturday nights, I would actually provide the entertainment myself. Sometimes my friend Egly would join me over the weekend, or my cousin Lenia, from my mother's side of the family, who was studying in London, would join us and we would put on a show of various Greek dances. The customers absolutely loved it. In fact, one summer, my aunt Georgina bought a piano for Egly to play in the Thanet restaurant, and we danced to our favourite Greek dances!

My *amour* Chris had a sister who lived and worked in Margate, and consequently he would spend his summer holidays working in his sister's restaurant to get some extra money. He never made the effort to meet me even though everybody knew that we liked each other, but we knew that if we were seen together then the gossip would start. He didn't take the initiative to express his feelings, apart from one time in Cyprus in the summer of 1972 just before I left Aradippou for London. In the end, it turned out to be the best outcome. He was quite selfish and not daring, unlike me. If I ended up with him, I would never have gone to America and my life would have been totally different, so I have no regrets at all. Besides, I didn't know then that I had already met the man who would become my husband.

As soon as I arrived in London in 1972, my cousin Ellou had introduced me to the woman who, unknown to me, was my future mother-in-law. Ellou said to me, 'I have a neighbour from Lefkara, and when I mentioned to her that you were coming to stay with me, she made me promise that I would take you over to her house so she can meet you.'

One afternoon in August, after I had spent a few weeks in London, we went to visit her neighbour Maria, and I met her son Philip, who was two years older than me. He seemed like a nice person, but at the time my mind was still on Chris. Philip was very polite and when we met a few times by chance while I was waiting at the bus stop to go to the LSE, we would talk and catch up.

While I was in Margate in the summer of 1974, the Greek army, with the agreement of the Cypriot EOKA-B group and at the behest of the Greek junta, declared a coup d'état and tried to overthrow the Cypriot Government. Archbishop Makarios III, the president of Cyprus, was overthrown, and everybody thought he had died, so for a few days, the Greek junta had control of Cyprus. However, President Makarios didn't die; he fled to his home village in Paphos and broadcast to the country that he was still alive and the legitimate President of Cyprus. Turkey found the perfect excuse and invaded Cyprus with the argument that they were coming to protect the Turkish Cypriots from the Greek army. The Americans gave the green light for the coup in Cyprus, and as a result of the Turkish invasion, the junta government in Greece was dissolved, and the Democratic Party took over the government. So ironically, Greece was liberated from military rule and Cyprus was divided, since Turkey occupied forty per cent of the island in the north during two rounds of warfare that led to many thousands of people, military and civilians, losing their lives or disappearing.

Because of the coup and subsequent war, I stayed in the UK that summer. I visited Cyprus the following year when things were more stable. That summer, many people who had British passports and were holidaying in Cyprus were evacuated and returned to the UK through the two British bases on the island.

Since I didn't have a British passport, if I had gone back home to visit my parents, I didn't know whether I would have been allowed to return to London. My sister Miroula and her family were caught up in the trauma, and they decided to emigrate to Australia with their two daughters, Tasoula and Effie. Miroula's husband Andreas had three brothers living in Adelaide and, as he was offered a job as a teacher, they decided to emigrate. They have since returned to Cyprus, but while they were in Adelaide and I was in Houston we used to write to each other on blue airmail paper in order to keep in touch.

Even now there are still missing people from the 1974 war, and every week we hear on the radio that more bones have been discovered. With the modern method of using DNA, they can identify the people so proper burials take place and there is closure for their families who have been living in hope that someday they would return. Cyprus is still divided, even today, almost fifty years later. It seems strange, for such a small island and a member of the EU to be so divided.

After I finished my degree and was getting ready to return to Cyprus in the summer of 1976, I bumped into Philip's mother Maria at Holborn tube station. I told her that I had finished my degree and was going back to Cyprus for the summer, but that I hoped my dad would allow me to return so I could do my MBA. She said, 'If you come back to London, come and see us,' and she kept on talking about her son Philip. I promised her that if I returned to London, I would visit her and catch up.

Christmas Eve at the Casino

When I finished university, I had to fight another battle with my father, to be allowed to stay for one more year in London. I wanted to go to the London Business School to do their two-year MBA course. In the meantime, my parents were very concerned that I was getting too old and I was still single; I was twenty-three, and everyone my age in Aradippou was getting married and having children. My two older sisters were married at eighteen and had children at nineteen, and my parents expected me to do the same. I reminded them that I had gone to England to study, not to find a husband; studying was my number-one priority. They told me that Neofytos – my cousin, who had studied at the LSE and then returned to Cyprus and got married to a lovely girl from Aradippou, Photoula – had a friend, a civil engineer who was working in Nicosia. He was from a good family in Paphos, well-off and very interested in meeting me. I agreed to meet Neofytos' friend, the civil engineer, but as soon as I met him, I knew if we got married it would not have lasted! He was very nice but too quiet; there was no way I could marry him. There was nothing wrong with him; he was well educated, OK-looking and from a good family, but my mind was still on Chris.

My parents had already arranged for me to go for job interviews in various banks in Nicosia. Egly and the other girls who had graduated from the LSE were also determined to do their MBAs. We were all able to get jobs in the local banks, since we were among the first female graduates in Economics from the LSE. We had offers from the biggest bank, the Bank of Cyprus, but we decided it would be best to go back to London and do our MBAs. Then, if we wanted, we could return to live and work in Cyprus. Personally, I was quite certain that I didn't want to return to Cyprus, but I kept that quiet for the time being and told my dad a white lie. I told him I would go back to England, and then come home at Christmas, get engaged and, once I finished my MBA, I would get married. I eventually compromised with my dad and went to City University, which became Cass Business School, and completed a one-year MBA rather than the two-year MBA at London Business School that was my preference. Finally, my dad said yes and I returned to London, but I never went back to live in Cyprus.

When I got back to London in September 1976, I kept my promise and went with my cousin Ellou to visit Philip's mother Maria. She was delighted to see us, and after the initial chat, she told us that Philip was on holiday in Greece. I found out later from him that he was away with his girlfriend. During that time, Philip was also under pressure to get married to a Cypriot girl, so they arranged for him to meet a number of eligible young women from the Cypriot community. He didn't like any of them, but his parents remembered that, when he first met me back in 1972, he had commented that he liked me. Thus, they decided to pursue the possibility of a union between Philip and me.

When Philip returned from his holiday, Maria told him that I was back in London and had visited her. The following week, Philip and his parents came to visit me. However, I was in Margate looking after my three cousins because my aunt Georgina was on holiday in Cyprus; every day I would finish my university lessons and take the train from Victoria Station to Margate. Ellou called me to say that the whole Patsalos family visited and were asking about me! She told them I was in Margate and that we could meet up when I returned to London.

Finally, Philip and I met again in late October. I had not seen him for a couple of years, and when I saw him again, I liked him. My cousin Kyriakos, Ellou's brother, who was now married to a Cypriot girl called Maro, was very involved in the Greek Cypriot Football League, and invited me and Philip to join him and his wife Maro at the Greek Dinner and Dance event in early November. We all had a great time and they both liked Philip. A couple of weeks later, Philip invited me for drinks at his house to meet some of his friends. Ellou walked with me over to his house and left. That was the first time I was meeting his friends, in particular his best friend Bunny and his cousin George. I found out later that he wanted them to see me and 'kind of check me out'! We all got along very well, and after everyone left, I stayed a bit longer and continued to talk, and Philip walked me home.

In the following weeks, Philip and I continued to meet regularly, but we were always chaperoned. It was getting close to Christmas. I knew that things were getting serious between me and Philip, so I discussed it with my friend Egly, who was returning to Cyprus to spend Christmas with her parents. Before she left, she told me not to rush into anything and to wait until the New Year before making any decisions. She knew that I had originally thought I might marry Chris, but he wasn't making any efforts or attempts to contact me and to discuss the possibility of a future together. When I had asked him about his plans a few months earlier and told him that my parents were putting pressure on me to get engaged, he still didn't make any positive commitment. At that point, I realised that he was an indecisive person and that I was better off without him.

A few days before Christmas, Philip called and asked me if I could go out with him for dinner on Christmas Eve, just the two of us, to the Playboy Casino in Park Lane, where he was a member. At that time, the Playboy Casino was the best and most fashionable place in London. I knew that he was very serious, so I talked to my cousin Ellou and her husband Stavros about my meeting up with Philip alone. Stavros suggested that it was best to call my dad and get his permission before agreeing to go out on my own with Philip. We called my father and told him what was unfolding, and he asked for Philip's full family name, so they could find out more about his family. Savvas, my brother-in-law, had spent time as a teacher in Lefkara, Philip's village, so he asked his contacts and friends about Philip's family. The responses were very positive, so I got the green light to go on a proper date with Philip.

He picked me up on Christmas Eve and we drove to Park Lane. Philip had the most up-to-date Greek songs playing in his car, and since I love Greek music, I was very impressed that he also liked it and kept on top of the latest hits. We chatted about various things, but in particular, he shared his plans of going to the US for a secondment at a medical school, so he could undertake his post-doctorate training. That was music to my ears, since I was fed up with living in London in the late 1970s under a Labour government, with such strong and uncontrollable unions that there were strikes all the time. In fact, we went through a period when, due to the strikes, we only had a three-day working week in order to preserve energy, gas and electricity. The marginal personal income tax rate was ninety-eight per cent and many people were emigrating to the US. The 'brain drain' had begun. I was very tired of living like this, so the chance to leave the UK for the US was like a siren's call to me! By the time we arrived at the casino, the atmosphere was more fluid and we felt more and more comfortable in each other's company.

As we talked over dinner at the Playboy Casino, we had started off by saying, 'I will do this and that,' when discussing our plans, but gradually the word 'we' crept in, until we were saying,

'We will do this and that,' as we talked about our future. We had a fantastic evening, and around midnight, we made our way down the beautiful wide staircase to the exit. As I started walking down, I froze. Philip asked me what the problem was, and I said that my father's first cousin Solomon, whom I had seen in Cyprus when he'd visited our home earlier that August, was coming up the stairs. He worked as a chauffeur for the Playboy Casino, driving all the big hitters to their hotels or homes.

As Solomon approached us, he recognised me and said, 'Hi, Eleftheria *mou*, how are you?' He then looked at Philip with a puzzled expression, and Philip immediately shook his hand and said, 'I am her fiancé.' So that's how Philip proposed to me!

My father's cousin congratulated us, and we left to go home and to tell Ellou and Stavros that we were now engaged. They were not surprised since they knew that Philip had serious intentions, so we all kissed and had champagne to celebrate. We agreed that on Christmas Day after the traditional lunch, Philip and his parents would come to Ellou's house to meet all the family – uncles, aunts, cousins and so on, and that's exactly what happened; all the family came over for lunch and they were so keen to meet Philip. My family really liked him, and we telephoned my parents to give them the good news and for my parents to speak to Philip.

Later that day, Philip and I drove to Alexandra Palace, a beautiful spot high up on a hill in North London, overlooking the whole of London. There, he kissed me for the first time, and I was so nervous I kept on laughing. After all, it was my first kiss!

A Village Wedding

Philip and I were engaged in February 1977 and my parents came from Cyprus for the engagement party. It wasn't a big party, just close family and friends. In June 1978, we went to Cyprus to get married and have a church wedding. My dad had told me, 'If you want to have the wedding in London, we will give you some money towards the party, but if you come to Cyprus, we will take care of all the expenses and still give you the money it would cost to have the wedding in London.' As I had always imagined myself getting married in Cyprus, we went for the second option.

1978 was still quite a difficult year, because a lot of people had lost family members following the Cypriot war with the Turks and my cousin Elli's husband was designated missing. The weddings immediately following the war, and for many years afterwards, were on a much smaller scale than they were before and indeed now. We had the wedding in Aradippou. I loved that I was getting married in my village. It was particularly exciting because I knew by then that we were going to America, so I felt very sentimental about Aradippou, knowing that I wouldn't be able to visit for a while.

Looking back, it was like that scene in *The Godfather* when they had the wedding in Sicily, and they walked to church with the violins playing. The groom would go first with his father, with the bride and her father walking behind them, followed by the rest of the family and friends. The whole village was invited to the wedding, which was traditional. The reception was held in my sister Youla's house, next to my parents' home. As it was a small event, only close family stayed for dinner, whereas before the war, the whole village would stay and weddings could go on for three days, starting on Sunday and finishing on the following Wednesday lunchtime. Our wedding was a small event compared to that, but it was still lovely.

On my wedding day, I was twenty-four, and my younger brothers, Takis and Nikos, were nineteen and seventeen. I had a beautiful full gown, which I bought in London with my cousin Ellou. My Cypriot friends from the LSE came, so I was surrounded by friends I had studied with. On the way to church, my mother kept telling me, 'Don't smile so much!' because a bride is supposed to be very demure, but I've always been an outgoing person. As the procession walked through the village to the church, I kept seeing my friends and saying hello to them as we went along, while my mother kept saying, 'Stop smiling!' Egly was my maid of honour and George Ellinas, Philip's cousin, was the best man. George came to Cyprus specifically to attend our wedding.

Philip and I went on honeymoon to the Greek Islands, which I had never actually visited before. We had originally planned to go to the Bahamas and even put down our deposit, eighty pounds, which was about a month's wages at the time. Unfortunately, we realised closer to the time that we didn't have enough money, and we didn't want to spend the money from our wedding since we expected to have a lot of expenses on our trip to America. Still, we had a fantastic time on our honeymoon. We stayed with my cousin Miroula and her husband Dinos in Athens for two nights and then we went to the Cyclades – Aegina, Spetses, Poros – and made friends with some other English couples, who were also newlyweds, that we met on the ferry sailing to the islands.

Back in the UK, the atmosphere was very depressing because of the political and economic instability. I finished my MBA in December 1977, slightly less than a year before we left for America. At the time when I was at the LSE, Margaret Thatcher was the Shadow Minister for Education, and she was preparing to impose substantial fees on foreign students attending universities in the UK. Whilst I was initially paying an annual fee of £250, the fees increased to £6,000 per year upon Margaret Thatcher's government gaining power. I got some exemption on the fees because my father's business had suffered during the war. At the time, there was a 'brain drain' in the world of academic research; many people were leaving to go to America, because there were no grants and everything was abysmal economically.

I got a job in a small knitwear company just off Regent Street, Adorence Company Ltd. My monthly net pay was just over a hundred pounds, and I used to spend most of it on clothes! The company imported beautiful knitwear from the Far East. Staff got discounts and samples and because we were near Oxford Street my colleagues and I would go shopping there. I was the assistant to the accountant, and I prepared the accounts for the auditors, worked on the leasing arrangements and factoring. I used to go to the Chemical Bank for all these transactions. All our merchandise came from China, Hong Kong, Taiwan and Singapore. I remember one of the most senior women in the marketing department where I worked was making £7,000 a year, which was a great deal of money compared to my annual pay! When I came back from America five years later, my first salary was over £10,000. Of course, by that time I was far more experienced, with a specialisation in US tax, but still, my salary was enormous compared to what I was earning before.

In 1973 I fell in love with playing tennis and I particularly enjoyed going to Wimbledon in the afternoon after college. Initially I was oblivious to tennis, but when Wimbledon matches started, usually in July, it didn't take long for me to become fixated with the sport. The summer after I arrived in London, my cousin Ellou went on holiday with her husband Stavros and left me in charge of the children, Mary, Chrisos, George and Eleftheria. We used to go to the local park, Broomfield Park, and play tennis. During our stay in Houston, when we were six hours behind London time, we used to get up early, prepare our breakfast and watch the Wimbledon finals on TV; the programme was entitled *Breakfast at Wimbledon*. We never missed it! When we returned to London, I continued going to Wimbledon, and I still go every year.

At the time, Philip was working in the pathology department at the National Hospital for Nervous Diseases (later the National Hospital for Neurology and Neurosurgery) in Queen Square. As I mentioned earlier, one of the things that attracted me to him while we were 'dating' – apart from the fact that he was good-looking – was that he wanted to go to America to do his post-doctorate training. Philip applied to several American institutions and medical schools. He was offered positions in Salt Lake City, Utah; in Houston, Texas; and in Pittsburgh, Pennsylvania. They were all excellent institutions, and it was not easy to choose which one to opt for. In the end we opted for Houston because at the time the show *Dallas* was on TV and very popular, and we were enthralled by *Dallas*. The mother on the show was called Miss Ellie. During my stay in London, my abbreviated name was Elfie, but eventually I dropped the 'F' and added an 'L'. My cousin Ellou's younger daughter was called Eleftheria, like me, and they called her Elfie, so I thought I would use the same name, but Philip never really liked me being called Elfie; he thought it sounded like *Alfie*, the film with Michael Caine. So, when we went to America, I became Ellie!

As there was no Internet in those days, I remember going to the local library in Palmers Green, which is still there, to see where Houston was on the map, and research the climate and what we needed to take with us. When Philip told his parents that we were going to America, they were very upset. He was an only child and helped them with their finances and everything they needed. They thought that if we went away, we would never return to London, and they were so upset that Philip had second thoughts. By that time, I couldn't stay in England any longer. My mind was set on leaving, so I said, 'Listen, I'm ready to go. If you don't want to go to America, then I'm leaving to go back to Cyprus. I can't tolerate the UK anymore, it's just dismal.' So, in the end, I was the one who pushed for us to go.

I have no real regrets, and I don't wonder whether anything could have been different. The only question mark I have over any part of my life is what would have happened if we hadn't gone to America. Just before we left for Houston, I had a job offer from the European Union (EU), who were looking for a Greek-speaking economist. Philip also had opportunities in Brussels; indeed later, when our children were finishing school, he was offered a job by a pharmaceutical company, but he turned it down because my career had taken off and Philip did not want to be distracted from his chosen area of research. I do wonder what my life would have been if I had taken the EU job – it was before Greece was part of the EU, which is why they were looking for Greek-speaking economists – but who knows? Our lives and our careers would have been very different. I might have been a member of Parliament in the EU, but that's not a regret so much, more of a 'what if?'. In any case, by the time I'd had an interview and they'd got back to me, we had already committed to go to Houston. I would never have changed my mind, and certainly never stayed behind, and it was good for Philip's career. We were both raring to go.

Miss Ellie in America

Houston was quite a shock to the system, but still very exciting. We arrived in Houston on 18th November 1978; I remember the date very clearly because the day after that, 19th November, was our first wedding anniversary (we still celebrate our civil wedding rather than our church wedding). Initially, we stayed with Philip's boss-to-be, Dr Richard Wiggins, and his wife Nancy, until we found an apartment close by. On our anniversary, we went out with Richard and Nancy to a Japanese restaurant. We flew to Houston on Braniff Airways via Dallas. When we got to Dallas, we had to change to a smaller plane, and I remember seeing a man with a huge Stetson hat, leather belt and cowboy boots. I thought, 'It's a different world!'

When we arrived in Houston, Richard and Nancy were waiting there for us with a sign saying 'Dr Philip Patsalos'. We enjoyed our stay with them; they were a very nice family and took good care of us. When we did find an apartment, we made sure that it wasn't too far away from them because they were the only people we knew in Houston. Nancy and I had our children at the same time, even though she was ten years older than me. They had both been married before and Nancy had a son called John who was seven years old at the time. We realised very quickly that most of the people we met were divorced. It turned out that this was much more common in the US than the UK at the time.

We couldn't take a lot of luggage with us since the weight limit was very low, so we sent most of our clothes by boat in tea chests. Our summer clothes didn't arrive until the following spring due to strikes at the ports in the UK. I put all my summer clothes into the tea chests and took my winter clothes with me, because it was coming up to December. However, Houston was very humid, so November and December were quite hot.

When I wanted to call my family in Aradippou from Houston, I had to go through quite a complicated process. At the time, there were only a few people who had telephones in their houses and my parents did not have a telephone. However, there was a public telephone in the central square of the village and I would call the village number and somebody in the square would pick it up, and then they would go to my dad's house and say, for example, 'Xenophon, your daughter in America is going to call you in an hour at the public telephone!' My parents would answer my call at the designated time. We exchanged news and it was wonderful to hear them talk to me and Philip. A few years later I was informed that a lady friend of the family had a telephone installed, so I arranged to call my parents when they were at her house. Later, more and more people in the village installed telephones in their houses, and although my dad was considering installing a telephone, he was worried about the cost. My dad was always cautious, since he had seven children and did not want to be too extravagant.

In Houston, Philip had a job, but I didn't; I had come over as an accompanying spouse, but being a housewife wasn't my style. When I started going to recruitment companies, the people who interviewed me were very sexist; because I was a newlywed, they were asking me if I had any plans to have children. Of course, I did, and you can't ask that these days, but back then, particularly in Texas, they didn't care. Philip was working at the University of Texas Medical School (UTMS), which was part of the Houston

Health Centre which encompassed several well-known hospitals, including MD Anderson, one of the top cancer hospitals in the world. The first time I accompanied Philip to the UTMS, we had lunch in the cafeteria and everyone, including us, ordered hamburgers. We picked up our knives and forks to cut into them, and then we realised that everyone else had picked them straight up with their hands! They were all looking at us, laughing and saying, 'What's all this? You're not in London anymore, you're in Texas!' After that, we ate our hamburgers like everyone else, using our hands! Later, we were told that MD Anderson Hospital had a vacancy in the accounting department, so I went for an interview. However, I told Philip I couldn't do it; it smelled of death, and it was just too depressing. Even though it was only a temporary position, I still couldn't work in that environment, so I continued to look for work elsewhere.

Nancy and Richard's neighbour worked at an oil and gas company, so he had contacts in that industry. His brother-in-law was working for another oil and gas exploration company called Rowan, and they were looking for someone in the tax department. He said to me, 'You have a background in finance and economics, maybe you would like to go for an interview?' I went for the interview and was offered the job in December 1978, and I started in the New Year. We had a car by then, a big green Pontiac LeMans automatic car. After I got the job, Philip would drive me to work, then pick me up at the end of the day and we went home together, since we didn't have enough money to have two cars and there was no reliable public transport system.

As a gesture of thanks to Richard and Nancy for hosting us when we arrived in Houston, and as thanks to their neighbours who'd introduced me to Rowan, I thought I would throw a dinner party for them. Richard and Nancy had been over to our apartment many times, but we hadn't had a proper dinner party as such since I wasn't much of a cook! I thought I would cook Greek food for my guests, and being naturally rather daring and optimistic, I chose the most difficult dishes to prepare. I decided to cook them *avgolemono* soup (an egg and lemon soup) and *dolmades* (stuffed vine leaves) with salad and potatoes. For dessert, I went to the Greek store and got ready-made baklava and some fruit and finished with the Greek coffee that I had brought with us from London, plus chocolates. The egg and lemon soup is very tricky to make; nowadays I know how to prepare it, but in those days, I had no idea. When you beat the eggs to add them into the hot soup, if you don't do it properly, it curdles like Chinese egg noodle soup, which is what happened to me. A good housewife would have been mortified to serve something like that! Of course, my guests didn't have a clue, because they weren't familiar with Greek food. Philip said to me, 'My God, what if they say something?' I just said to him, 'Don't say anything!'

Then I brought out the *dolmades*. When you prepare *dolmades*, you mix rice, mincemeat, lemon juice and spices, and you roll them in grapevine leaves, and of course you add oil and plenty of water for the rice to cook. I didn't add enough water with the oil, so the rice wasn't cooked properly; I could hear it crunching in their teeth as they chewed, so that was the second mistake. The desserts, thank God, were fine. I served the Greek coffee that was brewed on top of the stove, thinking – surely nothing will go wrong with this! While we had the coffee, I noticed that some of our guests were coughing and clearing their throats – I didn't pay too much attention until after they left, and I gathered up all the coffee cups. I noticed that they had drunk everything in the cups, including the sandy coffee grains at the bottom of the cup, which we called *pokathulia*. Greek coffee should only be drunk up to the grains in the cup, but they had drunk all of it; it was a disaster!

When I met our guests a few weeks later, I highlighted to them the whole series of errors; we just laughed, and they thanked me for the experience. I must say that my cooking got much better with time; practice makes perfect, so to speak. After that fiasco, I asked my sister Miroula to send me some recipes from Australia, where she lived at that time. I received them by airmail in those blue envelopes. I practised cooking those difficult dishes and slowly my cooking improved. Thankfully, my subsequent parties were much more successful!

Our first apartment was tiny, a first-floor one-bedroom flat. At the entrance was a small living room and a small kitchen/dining room. A door led to the bedroom and the en suite bathroom, and that was it. During our stay there Philip's old boss and mentor from London, Dr Peter Lascelles, gave a lecture at the hospital in Houston and, during his time there, visited us. When he arrived in our apartment, he said, 'Where's my bedroom?' and we had to say, 'There's no other bedroom!' but our sofa bed was very big and comfortable, so he was fine.

Rowan, the company I worked for in Houston, was an oil and gas drilling company. We worked for Shell, Exxon, Aramco and all the large global oil companies. The company owned huge drilling rigs which we leased to oil and gas companies, and provided the personnel employed by Rowan, whom we referred to as 'roughnecks'. I remember once we were having a new rig inaugurated in Louisiana. The rig was built by another company, Lafayette, and Rowan invited all the available staff and spouses to fly there on a Saturday in the company's plane to visit the rig. Philip and I accepted the invitation since neither of us had actually been on a rig before. We were struck by how huge it was, like a small town.

I had some very close friends at Rowan, including Wes Adams, who worked with me in the tax team, and Lori Degan, with whom we are still very good friends. My boss at Rowan and the head of the tax department, Glyn Wheeler, was very fond of the British, and he thought of me as English even though I had an accent that was definitely not British! He thought I knew everything about the UK, which was strange because when I lived in England, I knew I was considered a foreigner. At the time, the English people were not too welcoming to non-English nationals, and I always knew they did not see me as English.

Texans were very conservative, and it was Bible country, so the dress code at work was very strict. You had to wear tights – which they called pantyhose – all year round, including in the summer! I told HR that I just couldn't abide by that rule. Having been brought up in Cyprus, I was used to heat, but Houston was so humid. In the summer it was one hundred degrees Fahrenheit and one hundred per cent humidity. It felt like an oven, much worse than Cyprus. I said, 'If you want to fire me, that's fine, but I cannot wear pantyhose all year round. I'll put them on when it's cold.' They agreed, and from spring to winter I did not wear pantyhose, but to be excused from wearing them, I had to go through this whole complicated process with HR.

I loved music and dancing, and I craved Greek music. Houston, unlike New York, did not have a radio station that you could tune into in order to hear Greek songs and music. Philip's aunt had introduced me to the New York radio station when we went to visit her in December 1979, and it was so great being able to listen to the Greek language and to Greek songs on the radio, just like at home in Cyprus! In the UK, there were no such radio stations at that time. One night, back in Houston, Philip told me that the University of Houston was holding a Greek evening, as there were some Greek students in Houston. I was so excited. I said to Philip, 'Let's go, let's go!' That night, I danced so much, I could not stop – I was so excited to hear the music! My feet were stiff and killing me for days afterwards. Indeed, as our apartment was on the first floor, Philip had to carry me upstairs and I would descend on my butt. I was just so happy to hear Greek music again and dance!

Philip and I were newlyweds then, and we were keen to see as much of America as we could. We got in our big Pontiac LeMans car and travelled to the West Coast; we did not earn a lot of money, but we were young and free. In late September 1979, after we filed the company's US Consolidated Federal Tax Return, we went on a long trip to California. I read an advertisement in the paper that said, 'Idyllic timeshares available in beautiful north Texas. Attend a sales pitch and take a tour of the accommodation offered, and regardless of whether you purchase anything you get three nights' free accommodation at the Flamingo Hotel in Las Vegas.' Timeshares were very popular in those days; all you had to do was to show up and listen to the sales pitch and you would be gifted accommodation somewhere nice and exotic. In our case we had free accommodation at the Flamingo Hotel, a very nice hotel on the Strip in Las Vegas, Nevada. We had been planning to go to California anyway, so we decided to also visit Las Vegas. What we did not realise was that at the Flamingo Hotel we had to spend a whole afternoon listening to another timeshare (at a Las Vegas hotel) to validate our free accommodation at the Flamingo Hotel. However, it was a great experience full of wonderful memories.

We loved our journey across Texas to the border town of El Paso; it took a whole day of driving to complete the journey from Houston. After an overnight stay at a local hotel we drove through New Mexico, Oklahoma and then Arizona towards Las Vegas. In New Mexico, we went to Albuquerque and visited a museum dedicated to the history of the indigenous American Indians. Las Vegas was so amazing, all glitter and lights twenty-four hours a day! The Flamingo Hotel was very luxurious compared to the Motel 9 chain we used on the way to Vegas. Motel 9 hotels were a very cheap but clean and respectable chain, and we could book in advance of arriving at the new destination, so really, they were not bad at all for a cost of $9 per night!

From Las Vegas we drove all the way to Los Angeles, via the

wealthy and famous town of Palm Springs. Our plan was to stay a couple of days in Los Angeles, see the sights, take the Garden Route from Los Angeles to San Francisco and then come back to Texas via Colorado. Unfortunately, 1979 was the year when there was a shortage of petrol (gas) due to the war in the Middle East. We set off from Los Angeles on our way to San Francisco, but we couldn't find any gas stations that were open, and we were very low on gas, so we ended up staying overnight in our car in the car park of a gas station. In the morning we filled the car with gas and decided to return to Houston and abandon our plans to visit San Francisco and Colorado. People in the US regularly travel across the States using the extensive road network and thus there are many facilities that cater to travellers. For us, our road trip was a memorable and a fantastic experience all round.

Motherhood

My parents came to visit us in Houston while we were living in our small one-bedroom apartment, so we donated our bedroom to them and slept on the comfortable sofa bed. They were very impressed with Houston and Texas in general. As I mentioned earlier, my parents did not travel at all before I left Cyprus to study in 1972, but after visiting me in London, they got the travel bug, or to be honest my dad did. They travelled to many countries, including Greece, Australia and Spain, so it was quite natural that they would also visit us in Houston. My dad learned to get the local bus, which took him to the hospital where Philip worked, so he went there every day and from the hospital he visited the local zoo, where he spent quite a bit of time. My mum was happy staying home during the day until we returned home from work and went out for dinner and to visit friends. She loved to cook and help with the housework, and of course Philip welcomed her great Cypriot cooking.

During the weekends we visited sites such as the canals of San Antonio, the grand administrative building in Austin, the Capital of Texas and the NASA (National Aeronautics and Space Administration) facility located south of Houston. We also visited New Orleans and experienced that jazz culture and the wonderful Cajun food. It was so lovely having them with us. Philip's close friend Bunny and his then-girlfriend Claire also visited us from

London, as well as my cousin Jimmy, who was living in New York at the time. It was quite tricky since we were still in the small apartment, but we managed somehow and had lots of fun! When we visited NASA, I was fascinated to see the huge rockets that took the first men to the moon. We watched the films describing their journey with renewed fascination. I wondered what my sceptical grandmother would have made of all the artefacts associated with that first man landing on the moon! These visits reignited in me the desire to also travel into space, which is still a great desire of mine.

I remember very distinctly the first time we went to a proper American Thanksgiving celebration. As I mentioned earlier, during high school at the American Academy in Cyprus, we celebrated Thanksgiving, taking food to school to give to the poorer families, so we knew about the holiday. Still, our first experience of Thanksgiving was very special. Philip had a lot of friends and colleagues from the hospital, and we went to one of the girls' houses to celebrate the holiday and tasted the proper turkey and trimmings and pumpkin pie. The following Christmas, we drove with Richard and Nancy to Raleigh, North Carolina, where they were originally from. Philip drove our Pontiac LeMans car and we took in the sights in Alabama and through the Smoky Mountains. Richard had graduated from Duke University, one of the top universities in the US, and we visited Duke with its beautiful grounds. We also went to Chapel Hill University in Raleigh, another very well-known local university.

That year we had a proper American Christmas! We first visited Nancy's mother Hazel, a lovely woman. She was very clever, a Professor of Psychology at the local university. We also met Richard's parents, who were very nice and hospitable. We spent Christmas Eve with them at their house in Raleigh and Christmas Day at Hazel's house nearby. In total we stayed for five days. Philip and I were used to buying people one present each for Christmas, it was a cultural thing, and so we had wrapped one present per person. On Christmas morning we presented our one present to each person, and we were given at least ten presents each! We were so embarrassed, as we did not know the US custom of present-giving on Christmas Day! Following that visit, we continued to send Hazel and Richard's parents Christmas presents for years. During our visit to North Carolina, Richard, Philip and I drove to Washington DC for the day, since it wasn't that far. We saw all the sights and had a great day. Just after we got back to Houston, Nancy announced that she was pregnant, and shortly after that, I became pregnant with Maria. Kirsty was born in September 1980 and Maria two months later in November.

As our apartment was so small, and we did not really see the point in continuing to pay rent, we started looking for a house once I was pregnant. We knew Philip's mother would visit us when the baby was born, as well as other friends and relatives, so we thought it would be best if we had our own house. In the end, we bought a spacious three-bedroom house at a good price and with the potential of getting a good return on our money. We did not fully furnish the house because we knew we would not be staying long-term. We had always been expecting to return to London. We moved in late summer 1980, so I was heavily pregnant by that time.

Philip was away attending a medical conference in Kentucky with Richard Wiggins when Maria was born. We consulted my gynaecologist before Philip's departure and were given the assurance that the birth would be on time and in two weeks' time. Consequently, Philip embarked on the journey to attend his conference where he was to make a presentation. I continued to work up until the very last minute, as I was young and very fit – I was twenty-six – and in America at the time, when one went on maternity leave the paycheque stopped and we needed my salary to pay the bills. My boss said, 'Ellie, you're going to have this baby on the conference-room table!'

The weekend that Philip went to Kentucky my secretary, Cynthia, came to stay with me so I had company. Her family was very religious, so I remember we went to church that Sunday, then for lunch and then went for a walk. By the time we got home at six o'clock that Sunday night, my contractions had started.

I called Philip and said, 'It's happening.'

He said, 'No, it can't be. They said the baby will arrive on time, i.e., in two weeks' time. It must be a false alarm!' But Maria was impatient as usual, so she wanted to arrive earlier!

After a while, when the contractions became more regular and persistent and my water broke, Cynthia drove us to the Houston Memorial Hospital which was a few miles from our house. I called Philip when I was in the labour room and I said, 'It's definitely happening. Come home!'

By that time, it was very late on Sunday 9th November. The following morning Philip took the earliest flight available to Houston and arrived late in the morning. By then, I already had Maria. I gave birth to her at 6:01am on Monday morning, 10th November 1980. Richard announced to the attendees of the conference that the reason Dr Patsalos wasn't delivering his presentation was that he was on his way back to Houston to be with his wife and his new baby girl, so everyone at the conference clapped and knew that Maria was born before Philip had arrived!

My maternity leave lasted for six weeks. My mother-in-law, Maria, along with George, Philip's cousin, visited for a few weeks after Maria was born. We spent Christmas together with our newborn. George travelled on to Australia for New Year and returned to Houston in January, so he could return to London with my mother-in-law.

It was very exciting having a baby, but motherhood still took me by surprise. Maria was a very small baby, five pounds and ten ounces, and cried a lot; she had quite a strong character from a very young age. My mother-in-law held Maria all the time, whereas I was trying to get her into a routine. When she was bathed and fed, there would be no real reason to pick her up, but she would still cry, and my mother-in-law couldn't resist picking her up. By the time she returned to London, it was too late; Maria was used to being picked up and held all the time! Of course, I couldn't hold her all the time because after six weeks I had to go back to work. I remember we had a swing that we used to put her into, and she would fall asleep when she was in the swing, but when the swing stopped, she would open her eyes and start screaming again! We would continue swinging her until she fell asleep, and then we would put her to bed. She didn't sleep easily but she was a happy child and loved the good weather and playing out in the garden. We had to teach her to avoid the red anthills, which were very dangerous since the stings were very painful. We loved having her!

The following year my cousin Ellou, her husband Stavros and their daughter Elfie, plus Philip's dad, visited us. The most popular visiting areas in Texas were San Antonio with the famous Alamo and river walk, the seaside town of Galveston and Austin, the capital of Texas, but above all, everyone who visited us wanted to go to NASA and to New Orleans. It was after Apollo 9, so everyone was excited to visit NASA, which was about three hours from our house. After visiting NASA for the fifth time, I was tempted to say, 'Can we just show you the photographs?' Even for me, the excitement had subsided!

Our house was in a lovely new complex with a swimming pool and a playground for the kids. When Maria was a baby, I would take her around the complex, and later when she was older, we spent time in the swimming pool with other mums. Our new neighbourhood was very comfortable. It was called Bayleaf, and it was near Highway 59. We had a young Indian family living next door to us, and we became very close friends; when we visited Houston in 1996 with the kids, we visited our home and found out that our former neighbours had moved. We tracked them down, contacted them and managed to reconnect. It was lovely to see them again and their grown-up children whom we had known as babies.

Apart from the Indian family, we did not know many people and even though we had a good lifestyle, and of course the weather was much better than in the UK, we were quite lonely sometimes. All our friends, apart from Richard and Nancy, were younger than us and most of them did not have children. Lori and Wes were younger and neither of them was married at the time; they both got married after we left Houston. I progressed well in my company, and Philip was making good progress too. He was involved in interesting projects and publishing lots of research papers, an important part of his job, as well as teaching at the Houston Community College. By this time, I had not been back to Cyprus since we'd got married five years earlier, and we were thinking of going back to London to be closer to our families. I remember at the time of the Lebanese Civil War, we saw Larnaca and Limassol on TV because the Lebanese refugees escaped by boat to Cyprus. By then, I was pregnant with our second child Nicolas, and I did not want my children to grow up so far away from Cyprus. I said to Philip, 'We need to make up our minds.'

One day when Philip and I were walking around the neighbourhood I remember saying to him, 'Listen, we are not going to stay in the US. We must return to the UK.' We discussed it and agreed that the primary consideration was for Philip to get appointed in an established post within the medical fraternity and continue his work in the epilepsy field. I knew I was very versatile, so I could switch profession and find another job. At that time, Philip was actively looking for a job in academia in the US. We knew that if he was appointed to a new job, it would be difficult to return to the UK since he would be committed to the new job for at least five years. Most academics that went to the US did not return to the UK; it was a better lifestyle with more opportunities. Philip interviewed at various institutions including Washington DC, Louisville, Dallas, Galveston and Phoenix. We liked Phoenix because it was dry and hot, but it was a big decision because we knew that if we stayed in America and Philip became an Associate Professor, the next step in his career, we would stay in America forever.

In the summer of 1981, we visited London to have Maria's christening. We planned this visit to coincide with the wedding of my younger brother Chris, who was engaged to Pauline, a Cypriot girl living in Birmingham. They got married that summer and most of the family visited the UK to attend the wedding as well as Maria's christening. My parents, my brother Mitsios and his wife Youla came, as well as my brother-in-law Savakis, my sister Elli's husband and my lovely niece Eleni, who was studying in Thessaloniki, Greece. She was eighteen years old then. We had a big party for the christening, with a band and lots of singing and dancing. It was so great to see everyone after such a long time! We left Maria with my in-laws and drove to Birmingham for the wedding. We had a fantastic time with the celebrations and seeing so many friends and family whom we had not seen for so long! But our home was in Houston, and we were glad to get back.

Trees in the Swimming Pool

During the Christmas of 1982, while I was still pregnant with Nicolas, we visited London because Philip agreed to christen his first cousin Nick Nicholas's daughter Irenee, their first child. While in London Philip met his former boss, Dr Peter Lascelles, who had visited us in Houston, and he told Philip that there was a big possibility that a new position would be opening in his department with a two-year tenure in the first instance. The position would be at the National Hospital for Neurology and Neurosurgery, where Philip had worked before we moved to Houston. We were very excited by the prospect, even if the position was for two years; at least Philip would be settled, and he could explore other opportunities from London rather than from Houston or elsewhere in the US. We told Peter that we were very interested and asked him to keep us posted.

Nicolas was born on 18th January 1983, and while I had a tough pregnancy with Maria – I was sick for the entire nine months until I went into labour – with Nicolas it was easier. During my pregnancy with Nicolas, I didn't like to eat sweet foods, only savoury, and although I was hoping it would last, it didn't! I got my sweet tooth back fast once he was born. He was bigger than Maria had been, seven and a half pounds, and he ate lots when he was hungry, slept when he was tired; he was a very easy-going baby, and once fed and cleaned, he would fall asleep easily.

Still, having two children whilst living on our own was tough. It was especially hard once we had Nicolas as well as Maria, and when we were in the US, there was no one to relieve us. I stayed home for four weeks with Nicolas because, without a car, I was stuck in the house all day long. Philip was using our car to go to work since the public transportation system in Houston was essentially non-existent. Living in Houston was a great experience, but we missed our friends and felt quite lonely and isolated at times. Also, we were living there before my career really took off, so while Philip went to a few medical conferences, I only attended one course in New York, and apart from that I spent most of my time in Houston.

We got used to having a nanny in the US. Yolanda was a Cuban lady, very well educated. She was a community college teacher in Spanish, her daughter was studying medicine and her ex-husband was also a doctor. She really liked Philip and me and became like a second mother to us and, later, like a grandmother to the children; she loved them dearly. Sometimes, when Philip and I were too tired over the weekend, I would take the children to Yolanda's house, so we could sleep and rest for a couple of hours. I remember we went to Mexico City and Acapulco when I was pregnant with Nicolas – Philip had always wanted to go to Acapulco, after the Elvis Presley film *Fun in Acapulco*. We went for a week and left Maria with Yolanda, knowing she was in safe hands, but Maria was very upset because she thought we had abandoned her, so when we returned, she was very happy to see us!

Yolanda originally looked after Maria at her house, and when Maria was about one and a half, she opened her first nursery and first Maria started going there, and then Nicolas. Once Yolanda had opened her nursery, we dropped both children there in the mornings and after work, Philip would come to my office first and then we would pick up the children together in the car. Before I returned to work, Philip slept in one of the guest rooms so at least he got a full night's sleep, and after I returned to work, we used to alternate, so we each got a good night's sleep every other night.

Six months after Nicolas was born, we got the news from Peter Lascelles in London that the position was open, and Philip could return to work there, which was fantastic news for all of us. Even though we had loved our time in Houston, we both knew it was time to return home and Philip gave his notice in mid-August 1983. We were lucky twice with the economy in Houston. When we arrived, it was booming, but in 1983, as we were leaving, the oil price plummeted. As Houston depended heavily on the oil and gas industry, with the demand for oil going down so deeply and suddenly, it meant that the economy in Texas, and in particular Houston and Dallas, was very adversely affected. At Rowan, the price of the daily rate for a drilling rig was reduced to something like one-fifth of the price it had been when we'd arrived in Houston five years earlier due to the much lower price of the oil, so there was no demand for more oil drilling. All around us, we saw people walking away from their home equity and losing their money, and we started to get concerned that we might not be able to sell our house. In the end, we were lucky; we got a buyer who returned with his family to Houston from Saudi Arabia after his job there ended. The exchange rate, dollar to pound, was also very good for us, because upon our return to London, we had dollars which were strong compared to British pounds.

After we sold our house, we had two weeks before we were due to leave the US. We stayed for a week with my friend Wes Adams and for another week with Joachim, a German colleague of Philip's. Just before we left, a hurricane hit, and the eye of the hurricane came through Houston. Living in Houston, we were used to big storms and strong rainfalls. During hurricane warnings we had to put tape on our windows at home, and at work, we ensured that all the important documents were moved to safe places and away from the windows. It seemed ironic that it was only during our last week in Houston that we witnessed the eye of the hurricane pass through. Thankfully, there were not many fatalities, but we witnessed first-hand what a hurricane was, and it was very scary! The rain was lashing the buildings, and the trees were leaning back and forth onto the ground before being uprooted – most of the trees in Joachim's garden were uprooted or broken and fell into his swimming pool. During our stay, there was no electricity, which meant no air conditioning, and of course Houston being very hot and humid meant that it was very uncomfortable. I remember being there with Maria and the baby, looking at those trees swinging, and thinking, 'God, couldn't you have waited another week?'

Also, during our stay with Joachim, I discovered a lump in one of my breasts, which scared me. Philip was in London, having used Rowan's aeroplane to take some of our belongings to London ahead of us, so I was on my own. When I told him, he was very concerned, so I had an operation to remove the lump. Thank God, it turned out to be benign, but that was my first encounter with breast cancer.

On 5th September 1983, during the US Labor Day celebrations, a holiday for everyone in the US, we boarded the plane and returned home. We had a number of leaving parties at Rowan, at the hospital and at our home before we sold it. We had a few garage sales to get rid of many things we'd accumulated during our stay, gave away all the liquor which Philip didn't drink and off we went. It was very sad but the right thing to do. We were very excited going back to London, knowing that our children would grow close to their grandparents, and we would also be able to visit my family in Cyprus more often. We had loved Houston, the place which had helped Philip and me to mature and be more confident, but we knew it was time to say goodbye.

America opened our eyes and fuelled our ambitions and confidence. American people believe that anything is possible, and their children are brought up in a way that gives them confidence from a very young age. In the UK, it's very different and people don't have this type of confidence. In America you are told that, no matter who you are, if you work hard you can get to the very top. You can even become President! It's a different way of life. You can see some of it in American movies, but if you haven't lived there, it's hard to understand. We are very fortunate that we lived in that world and experienced it, because it was very important to me. America made me stronger and gave me the additional oomph and confidence I needed. I learned a lot while I was there, so when I returned to London, I was comfortable in my knowledge.

Upon our return to London in September 1983, we stayed with my in-laws. At the time, my mother-in-law was working as a finisher in a Greek Cypriot-owned clothes factory, and Philip's father was a chef in a big restaurant in Central London, before he moved locally to manage a fish and chip shop in Fox Lane, North London. They didn't make much money, but they were very conscientious about their spending. They managed to buy a house in 1968, and in those days, we knew very few people who owned their own house. They started off by renting a couple of rooms in Kentish Town, and then they moved to Palmers Green, where their house still belongs to our family. They bought that house for £5,750; it was a different era! Philip's mother had missed her grandchildren, and she was more than happy to take early retirement; we helped her by paying her wages, and she looked after the children as well as cooking for us. Six months later we bought our own house and Philip would drop off the kids in the morning with my mother-in-law and pick them up after work in the evening. By the time they were picked up, they were fed and ready for their bath before going to bed. That was a huge help, since I didn't have to worry about them.

My in-laws' house had two rooms downstairs, a kitchen, three bedrooms upstairs, and a bathroom and toilet. We stored all our furniture and belongings that we sent from the US in the downstairs back room. By then we were used to our own house and independence, so it was tough living with my in-laws, because Maria and baby Nicolas were in our bedroom, and we only had the one room downstairs where we would all sit together to relax and watch TV. We started looking for a house as soon as we were back in London, but the prices were much higher than we'd anticipated. With some financial assistance from my parents and my in-laws, we were able to purchase our first house in January 1984 in Winchmore Hill, a lovely semi-detached house with four bedrooms and a nicely sized garden, where we stayed for eight happy years while the children grew up.

A Circle of Friends and Family

When we came back from the US, Maria was two and a half and Nicolas was a ten-month-old baby. We already had an existing circle of friends and family in the UK, and that circle expanded once we were living there permanently again. I had my cousins - Ellou, Kyriakos, Nicos, Maroula and Vasilakis - from my aunt Chryssi, my mum's older sister. I also had the other Ellou, Neofytos' sister, the daughter of my aunt Stavroula who was living in Cyprus but sadly died while I was in Houston, at the relatively young age of sixty. There was also my aunt Georgina and uncle Louis in Margate, with whom I had stayed as a student, but we had not really seen her family very often except for Tony and his wife Helen, who lived in London at the time. Tony later assisted me in finding Philip during the 7/7 terrorist attack in London, and Helen was my hairdresser for several years before they moved back to Margate.

After we returned, I got to know Philip's first cousin Nick Nicholas and his wife Eve very well. Their daughter Irenee, whom we christened on a trip back to London while we were living in Houston, is a little younger than Maria, and their second son Sotiris is a similar age to Nicolas. They also had a third child, Katerina. I met Eve's brother Aris and his wife Niki through Eve, at Irenee's christening. Niki has five sisters, and we became friends with Stavroula and George, Liz and Louis, and Thea and Chris. George was a senior partner in an accounting firm in London, so we had a lot in common. Louis was in fashion and had a factory producing fashionable clothes, so I frequented his factory and loved wearing his clothes, but Niki was closer to me. We had the same temperament! Her eldest daughter Kerri is the same age as Maria, her son Nicholas is a bit younger than my Nicolas and she also has a third child, Zoe, a similar age to Katerina.

Philip had another first cousin, Elli Pashourtides, who was married to Ortho, and they had three children, Lucy, Vangelis and Nicholas, who were also younger than our children. Because of those connections and because they went to the same Greek school, the kids grew up together in an extended family circle. Philip had no brothers and sisters, so his cousins were like brothers and sisters to him, and our children treated their children as cousins too.

At Greek school we also met Tasoula and George Charalambous. Their eldest daughter was also called Maria, and she was a little older than my Maria, but my Maria was further ahead in terms of her Greek, so she was in the same class as Maria Charalambous. We also met Laki and Ephie Tryphonides. Their eldest son Nicholas was the same age as Maria, but because my Nicolas was also more advanced in Greek, he was in the same class as their Nicholas! The other boy that Nicolas met during his childhood was called Steph Nicholaou, and the three of them remained friends throughout their lives and were best men at each other's weddings. We also got to know Steph's parents, Maria and Nick, so the Greek school also facilitated the expansion of our friendship group.

We were also friendly with another couple when the children were young, Andy and Androulla Georgiou. Andy was at the same high school as Philip, and it just so happened that our first house was around the corner from theirs. Their children Victoria and Alex were a little younger than our two, but they were all similar ages and they all played together in the alleyway near our house on their bicycles. I christened Alex, so the bond between our families became even stronger. Later, Andy and Androulla relocated to Paphos in Cyprus.

This period of our lives was very exciting – we were younger, the kids were growing up and our family would go on wonderful holidays together; we went to Cyprus every year, because we had my family there, but after the kids were in their teens, we travelled further afield, to Dubai, Australia, the US and South Africa. Through Andy and Androulla, we met a lovely couple, Olympia and Andreas Constantinou, who lived around the corner from us in Winchmore Hill and we are still very close friends.

When I was at the LSE with my cousin Neofytos, one of his very close friends was called Lambros Varnavides. When I met Lambros one day at Liz's house, I realised I knew him from our college days. He was older than me and Philip but part of the same circle, and he was married to Katie, who has three sisters, so the two sisters who lived in London became part of the group, Mary and Phaedra. In addition to all these friends, through Stavroula Michaelides, we met a number of other couples: Dia and Tas Anastasi, Martha and John Behiri, Mandy and Harris Hadjipapas, Despo and Kikis Zinonos, and Liana and Harris Pattihis. Through Niki and Aris, we met Dem and Stav Aresti. Dem was Aris' first cousin. Furthermore, we met Ismini and John Demades and through them, Andry and Costas Tsentas. Through my niece Eleni, we also met John Ioannou. They were introduced in Cyprus when they were both single and liked each other. However, in the end, they went their separate ways, but we kept in close contact with John, and he introduced us to his twin brother Peter. At that time, the twins were involved in the lucrative computer business, so we introduced them to Philip's close friend Bunny Georgiou, who was involved in computer programming. They all worked together, and they are still close friends. When John and Peter married, we met Anna and Yioda, their respective spouses. We are still very close friends. Basically, the group kept expanding all the time!

When the children were younger, we didn't go out that much. It was easier to have dinner parties in each other's houses, and during that period, we came up with the idea of creating a gourmet dining group to make the dinner parties a little more fun and interesting. The core group was made up of four couples – Nick and Eve Nicholas, Elli and Ortho Pashourtides, Niki and Ari Aresti (Eve's brother), and us. We set up this gourmet group called the NAPP, which was the initials of all our surnames – Nicholas, Aresti, Patsalos and Pashourtides. The intention of the group was that the couple that hosted the dinner would provide the main course and drinks. The other three couples would in turn provide the starter, the vegetables, salads and potatoes to accompany the main course, and the desserts. Sometimes we invited a guest couple, and sometimes two guest couples to make it more exciting – it was all great fun. It was agreed that the host took minutes of the unfolding evening, which were read out at the subsequent dinner, and we used them to make fun of each other and of our guests! Every six weeks, we would hold one of these dinner parties, and at the end of the year, we had a NAPP Christmas party. We invited all our guests for the year, sometimes with an extra honorary couple, and the men all wore black ties and tuxedos and the women dressed up. It was a fantastic event! It was for grown-ups only; the children were always in bed by that time. It continued for several years before gradually fizzling out, but while it lasted, everybody wanted to be invited to the NAPP dinner parties.

As I've said before, I'm not a very good cook, but the challenge of the NAPP was that you had to prepare something original that you had never prepared before. I never had time to try anything new, whereas Eve and some of the other girls would make a big effort every time. Eve was a housewife, whereas Niki was like me, less interested in cooking than Eve, who practised beforehand, creating elaborate dishes such as Beef Wellington. Niki was also very good, even though she did not want to spend too much time in the kitchen, and even now she is a very innovative cook. I have some very good recipes from her. The NAPP gatherings forced us to think about what we were making, especially as once you decided on the main course you had to inform the others what you were making to ensure their vegetables and starters would complement the main course. It forced me to be more daring and take more time thinking about what to cook and getting good recipes from others to impress the group. Once a year, we voted between the four couples whose dish was the best main course, starter and dessert. I won one year – it was very unusual because I had apparently made a winning dessert and usually preparing a dessert was worse for me than anything else. Maybe they were being kind because I wasn't all that interested in cooking; I was always far more interested in the social side!

During those years, in addition to my personal events, I had all the responsibilities of my corporate life, such as entertaining clients, attending many events and not being in London very often meant that I had to be very disciplined in planning things well in advance, so I always had my dinner parties between my trips. I continue to be socially active, and in 2018, I organised two dinner parties in June – same menu for two different groups of twelve guests. Once you do one menu it's easy to replicate the following week, which I did! I always get somebody to help me with the *hors d'oeuvres*, whether they are English or Greek delicacies which are difficult to prepare, and some special sweets. For many years, I had dinner parties comprising of twenty-four guests. I would move the furniture around and have twelve guests in the informal living room and twelve in the dining room, with drinks in the formal sitting room. The rationale of having so many guests was that I felt that if you were cooking for twelve, you end up really cooking for twenty-four anyway, and the more people you invite, the more social obligations you can get through in one night. I have stopped that now because I realised that you don't have time to sit next to everybody and have in-depth conversations, and you run around like crazy all night, so I decided twelve is now the best option. It's just homelier and more intimate when you can all sit around the dining table, even if it means more work having two dinner parties on consecutive Saturdays!

Finding My Feet

When I came back from the US, I knew what I wanted. I wanted to make a life in London, buy a nice house and get a job I would enjoy, though I never dreamt that I would reach the level in my career that I achieved. As soon as we got back, I was working, charting my career and going up the ladder. I decided early that this was what I wanted to do. I didn't care what anybody might say. All my close Greek Cypriot friends were housewives, and I was the only one from our circle who worked, but I never felt strange about that. Philip and I realised that my career would be the more important one in the family, because that's where the money was.

When we returned from Houston, we were not very knowledgeable about schools, public or private. Since our children were very young, the first thing to look for was a nursery school for Maria. The closest one to Philip's mother and father was a local Church of England nursery, so Maria started going there. Later, Nicolas joined that nursery when he was around three years old, and when Maria had to go to school, we applied to the Church of England School, St Paul's, which had an excellent reputation and was close to our home. Maria had to go for an interview and did very well, perhaps an indication of what was ahead of her. She started school there and was very happy.

When I first started interviewing for jobs in London, I didn't know that you could work in an accounting firm if you were not a chartered accountant. I was an economist and an MBA in International Law and Marketing, so I did not think that was an option for me. After several interviews through a headhunting firm, I got a job at Ernst & Whinney (now Ernst & Young) in the US tax department. In 1983, the oil and gas sector was dead. Since my tax experience was in that sector, I applied to a lot of oil and gas companies, but there were no opportunities because the price was still down, so they were not hiring. The only chance I had was to change my focus from US corporate/international tax to personal tax. There was very little demand for US corporate tax in the UK in those days, so I had to start at a lower level to build up my knowledge.

Also, I was a foreign woman with an accent. In those days, the accounting world was very much dominated by men. This was more the case in audit than tax, but still, I had to struggle hard to differentiate myself from all the others. I started as an associate, the lowest level, because I didn't know anything about personal US tax; I had been involved on a very limited basis during my time at Rowan, when we used to assist our US employees with their filing obligations in the US while they were working overseas, but I had not done much more than that – and my own US tax returns, of course. Still, by 1987, I was made an assistant manager, working on both corporate and personal tax.

I had discovered other passions in America: being fit, going to the gym and running. I had been running since before I came back from America in 1983. As a child, I was always mischievous, always out and about, because we didn't have TV, so we had to make our own entertainment. When I was studying in the UK, nobody went to the gym, unless you were on a team – rugby, football or basketball – it wasn't the done thing. When I started being very aware of the importance of exercise, it was in the US. I started exercising properly in Houston after I had Maria, in 1980

– so that's about forty years, a long time. When I came back from the US, I was lucky to meet my dear friend Lynn Leigh at Ernst & Whinney. She is an American, but she married a British lawyer she met while they were both climbing in Chile. We were both into running, so we started running together at lunchtime. Those were also the days of the aerobics craze, so we would go to the Pineapple Studio in Covent Garden for the advanced aerobics classes – we had the big hair, crop tops and leggings, which were very much the in thing during the eighties! After we came back to live in the UK, we would go on holiday in August to Cyprus, and of course, it was very hot. My dad was very confused by my running in that heat, and he said to me, 'Only fools run for no reason!' It was not customary back then, but I never stopped.

During one of our tax training courses outside London, Lynn and I ran initially only for short distances, and then for longer and longer. When we returned to the office, we told our close colleagues that we were running during our lunchtimes, and they also volunteered to be part of the group. Six of us started running every lunchtime across the Embankment, past the Royal Festival Hall, across to St James's Park and around the opposite side to Vauxhall Bridge and back to our offices, Becket House, opposite St Thomas's Hospital. If the weather wasn't good for running outside, we started running up and down the stairs of our eight-floor building. Initially it was tough and for a few days we couldn't move our legs at all because we used muscles that we had never used before! But after a while, we got better.

The following May our group decided to run the City's prominent half-marathon and I was determined from day one that I wanted to finish in less than two hours, so I could get a medal! We all intensified our running, both together as a group and separately. I bought a speedometer to check how many minutes per mile I ran and tried to do better. I ran a few long-distance runs over the weekend, and the kids and Philip were great supporters.

When the big day arrived, it was a lovely spring day; not too hot, just perfect. I ran the race with confidence, finished after an hour and fifty minutes, and received my medal! Philip, Maria and Nicolas came to Hyde Park and watched me. They cheered loudly when I passed by them, and I was so happy to see them! I was so proud of my medal that for weeks afterwards I carried it with me and was telling everyone about my achievement. By this point, Maria was getting embarrassed and begged me to put it away. I listened to her and put my medal in the study – in a prominent position, of course. I came across it in the study recently and it brought back lovely memories!

1987 was a critical year for me. I was working very hard, including over the weekends during the busy season (March to mid-June), and learning about the US expatriate tax specialty. In early 1987, my colleague Jean del'Achai, another American lady who was more junior to me, who transferred from audit to tax and was working with me on several of my clients, left Ernst & Whinney and joined a smaller accounting firm, Spicer & Pegler. After the Big Eight firms at that time, S&P was the top of the second tier of accounting firms. It had an excellent reputation for its tax department, serving all the City firms from merchant banks to law firms. Jean and I had agreed to keep in touch, and one day out of the blue, she called me and mentioned that S&P had a role which she thought was just perfect for me. Jean said that they were looking for someone experienced to set up and lead their new expatriate tax department. This was a very timely opportunity because by spring 1987, I felt that I had learned all I could from my current role, and it was time for me to move to somewhere new and advance my career. I was interviewed by Julia Le Blan, who was then a senior manager, and Ian Watson, Partner in charge of the Financial Services Tax Group. They loved me and offered me a job as assistant manager – a real step up from the supervisor role I had at Ernst & Whinney, with a £10,000 pay rise.

Wow, that was it – the real beginning of my career progression upwards and upwards! Although I was petrified by the challenge, after much encouragement by Philip, I accepted. Years later, Julia Le Blan worked closely with me on the Bloomberg account when I was the lead partner.

During my transition into the new role, I counted myself very lucky to have Philip because he was my rock. If I had married a typical Cypriot man who had no appreciation of what it meant for me to continue to work, and he insisted that I had to stay at home and look after the kids, I would have died – well, to be honest, I would have had to divorce him. But right from the start, Philip and I were a partnership, and he always encouraged me. This brings me to the third most important moment in my life, and that was marrying Philip! He has always been my biggest fan, encouraged me to take on more responsibility, and trusted me during the years of constant travelling for business. Without his and his parents' support, I couldn't have achieved what I managed during my professional career! Initially, when I first joined Spicer & Pegler, I was not only doing compliance – tax returns – but also consulting – tax advisory – and I wasn't very confident in letter and document writing, so Philip would check and correct them. After a while, I was just fine, but it was that support and encouragement that he provided, and that continued confidence he instilled in me. He would always say, 'You can do it.'

Work was challenging as well as rewarding. I was very pleased to have been able to grow my career, but my role changed from one day to the next. I was getting double the salary, and so, of course, they expected more from me. The relentless travelling, going around the world, was another obstacle for a woman in those days, as most of the women I knew stayed home and looked after the kids. Among all my friends in the Greek community, I was one of the odd ones out in that crowd, because everyone stayed at home. One day when Maria was in primary school, she said, 'Mum, why are you not around after school so I can bring my friends over for tea? My friends invite me to go to their homes, but *yiayia* (grandmother) doesn't drive so I cannot accept their invitations.' She asked why I was never home to provide her with a cooked meal, and why she had to go straight to *yiayia* when she finished school.

I said to Maria, 'Mummy works, and the reason why we have this big house, and the cars, and all the holidays, is because Mummy works. And you know that if I stayed home, I wouldn't be happy.' That was the only time she asked me that. Sometimes I would miss their sports day if I was travelling overseas or I couldn't get away, but I managed to make it work. I attended all the school parents' evenings, and the Christmas plays and celebrations. The dates were always in my diary, and I would prioritise as much as I could. If I couldn't, it was often because I was away. Nowadays, I see a lot of myself in Maria. She is very clever, good at multitasking – sometimes I feel like she knows everything! When I was her age, I was on top of the world, climbing the corporate ladder very fast, and I can see that in her – the thrill, the excitement of getting new work and being appreciated, going from strength to strength. I know that she loves it and thrives on it too.

A year or so after arriving in London, we got to know the grown-up children of my cousins, including Stav (Stavroula), Ellou's and George's oldest daughter, who had just finished her course and was ready to settle down. After some deliberation, Philip told me that he thought that the brother of his very close friend Bunny, Bambos Georgiou, could be a suitable young man for Stav. So, after some elaborate planning which included my cousin Ellou and Bambos' mother Anthoula, we organised a blind date meeting in our house, one Sunday afternoon. Neither Bambos nor Stav had any idea about our plan. But the meeting was successful! They liked each other and, in the spring of 1984, they were engaged. I was the maid of honour at their wedding.

We are still very close with them and with their three lovely daughters, Elena and the twins Raphaela and Sophia. In fact, I christened Raphaela while Ismini Demades christened Sophia. But for Philip and me, both girls are our goddaughters!

Treatment

In March 1987, my cousin Neofytos' wife, Photoula, was diagnosed with breast cancer and had a unilateral mastectomy. I was very upset, of course, because I knew her well, but I also had something else on my mind. I said to Philip, 'You know, I haven't had a mammogram since 1983 when I had the lump removed while in Houston.'

Back in 1983, in our last weeks in Houston, I was having a shower and I found a lump in my breast. As I said before, we had two weeks in Houston between selling our house and moving back to London. We stayed one week with my colleague Wes Adams, and one week with Philip's colleague Joachim – that was the time of the hurricane, where all the trees fell into his swimming pool. I was on my own with the children at the time. Rowan, the oil and gas company I worked for, had operations outside Aberdeen. Rowan's employees worked in North Sea Oil; they had two weeks on and then two weeks off. At the beginning of the month, the plane would take the new crew over and bring back the other crew. The week I found the lump, Philip had gone to the UK on the company plane, taking suitcases and other personal belongings before we moved. When I told Philip, he was very concerned and came back as soon as he could. I had an operation, and the doctor took the lump out to analyse it. I had always had quite lumpy breasts ever since I was young, so it was a relief when the results came back, saying the lump was benign.

In March 1987 I was working for Ernst & Whinney at Becket House, opposite St Thomas's Hospital, so it was convenient to make an appointment there for a mammogram. I was quite relaxed, expecting the results to be fine. However, when the results came out, I was told to go and see Mr Anthony, a surgeon, at the oncology department. He told me that they had found a very tiny form of cancer, about the size of the head of a pin. Mr Anthony told me that I was lucky that they had seen it because it was so small, and if the person who performed the mammogram had been less experienced, they would have probably missed it. As it was so tiny, they told me there was no need for chemotherapy, but they recommended I should start radiotherapy. I started on a course of radiotherapy, and Lynn Leigh, my colleague, covered for me. Nobody knew apart from Lynn and Philip. I began going regularly to radiotherapy sessions in March 1987, and after I finished the course in June, the doctor told me, 'There's nothing to worry about.'

That summer, the whole family went to Cyprus because my youngest brother Nicos was getting married to Leoni and my daughter Maria was to be a bridesmaid – Nicolas was still too young to be in the wedding party. I had planned to have my tubes tied when we came back in early September. I did not want to have any more children, because of the breast cancer scare – they asked me if I was sure about not having more children, but I told them I was very sure. I was admitted to hospital in late September to have this procedure, and while I was in the hospital, they found a little lump in the centre of my chest. They didn't know what it was, so they said at first, 'Oh, maybe we should take it out as well,' but while I was there, something else appeared on my breast. The doctors panicked; they thought that the cancer must have moved from one breast to the other. They suggested a double mastectomy, and Philip and I agreed to it – there was no double-checking or second opinion. We were so scared and breast cancer was quite rare at the time, so we did not know that much about the disease and our options. Over time, Philip thought that they had possibly overreacted, and I had not had breast cancer at all, but years later it turned out that this was wrong because my tests showed I had the BRCA-2 gene mutation. Philip's parents knew something was happening, but we said it was some sort of problem with my tubes, something gynaecological. They never knew that I had a double mastectomy.

By December 1987, before Christmas, I had the operation. It was quite traumatic, but my work kept me going. I remember when I was having the different tests before the operations, such as a bone scan, I was still going from meeting to meeting. To me, my work was a saviour. I only stayed at home for a week when I was too sore to put my coat on. In those days, there was no breast reconstruction. A few years later, I was told that I could be evaluated to see if reconstruction was right for me, so I went to Hammersmith Hospital, and what I saw there was just horrendous. I said, 'No way.' They showed me some frightful photos of women who had the reconstruction, and it all just looked so awful and unnatural. Another big problem was that because I was always quite slim, I did not have a lot of muscle around my stomach and the operation would have meant that they would have had to take more muscles from my shoulders. Also, even though it was my own tissue from the same body, it was a very serious operation, and any graft could still be rejected. When they informed me that my back would end up scarred, I told them that I was staying just the way I was.

Sometimes people still ask me about breast reconstruction. My friend Marigay recently told me that she knows a surgeon who does a wonderful job in similar cases. She mentioned my case to him, and she told me that he said he would be happy to see me. I said, 'Marigay, what's the point? My youth is gone, and Philip and I are used to it, so really there is no problem!' At the time, I was still shocked and surprised by what had happened to me. The funny thing was that after I was diagnosed with breast cancer, I thought, 'Oh God, if I die, they will have to get rid of all my clothes!' The hardest thing was in the summer, especially when we went on holiday in Cyprus because I had always worn lovely clothes and bikinis. I wondered what my sisters would say when they saw me in high-cut tops and bathing suits, but they didn't say anything. I had to tell them what had happened, and they said, 'Yes, we wondered why you were not wearing the usual bikinis.'

After the operation, during the first two years, I went twice a year for a check-up, then annually for the next five years. I was taking tamoxifen; this drug was very good for post-breast cancer operation patients. I took the drug for seven years, and then after those seven years were up, I was informed that there was no need for any further follow-ups, and I was discharged. They told me about the correlation between breast and ovarian cancer, and I had a couple of follow-up appointments, but everything was fine, and after that, I just forgot about the danger and got on with my life. As there were no breasts, there was no possibility of the breast cancer recurring, and I felt very lucky that my lymph nodes were not affected because the cancer was caught very early.

At the time, Philip was the one who was the more emotionally impacted. He was the one who did not want me to say anything to anybody. I still don't know why I agreed with him, but I was also convinced that some people had to know what happened. For several years, I didn't tell anyone apart from Lynn Leigh, who was aware of what happened to me from the very beginning. After a few years, I told Eleni, my oldest niece. We were best friends – Eleni knew all my personal issues and I knew all of hers. After Eleni, I told my good friends Maro and Egly and then my sisters.

The children did not know. Maria told me later that sometimes in the garden, my top would slide down and she would see the wound, but she did not question anything at the time; it was only later that she really understood what had happened. My friends and family were horrified to find out what had happened, but because it had been a few years by the time I told them, and I was fine, it was easier to accept.

It was a good thing that I told Eleni because later she was diagnosed with breast cancer herself, and if she hadn't been aware of my case, they might not have taken it as seriously. Like me, she was quite young when she was diagnosed – I was thirty-three and she was thirty-five, but unfortunately, she had a very aggressive form of cancer. She did not want to have a mastectomy, and by this time the doctors were more reluctant to perform immediate mastectomies. I kept telling her to go for it, but the doctors told her that it wasn't absolutely necessary. They suggested they would remove the whole lump and area around it, and then give her an aggressive form of chemotherapy. However, after a couple of years, the cancer came back and spread to other parts of her body. She fought it for a long time, and she came to London for treatment many times. It was so sad, such a beautiful, active, talented girl with so much to give. I relived everything, all the pain, through her. It was a tough period!

During this time, as well as the progress in my career and upheavals in my health, I lost my mother. The year after my younger brother Nico got married, we went to Cyprus in mid-July for the traditional four weeks' vacation with the kids. My mother, as always, looked after us, cooked and cleaned. They were harvesting the olives at the time and had a lot of women helping them, sifting through to segregate the olives that would go to the olive press factory and putting them into sacks. In October, my mother was unwell, and she went to the doctor, where a biopsy was taken. Everything came out all normal, but as it turned out, the doctor had biopsied the wrong site. By December, my mother was diagnosed with cancer (non-Hodgkin's lymphoma), which by that time had spread. My mother and father came to London in January for a second opinion, but the tests and scans confirmed that she had an aggressive lymphoma. They were advised to return to Cyprus for chemotherapy, and by the end of the summer, on 4th September 1991, my mother died. In early August, I had taken the children to Cyprus to spend some time with her as she was in remission. While I was in Cyprus, my mother was admitted to hospital and the doctor told me and the family that she still had quite some time, so I flew back to London – but within a week, she was dead, and I returned to Cyprus to attend the funeral. It all happened very fast. She was diagnosed in October, and she died the following September. My father was much older (eighty-eight) when he died, but my mother was only seventy, which was young, even by the standards of the day.

Looking back on my own illness, I never cried, never gave in to doom and gloom. I was very pragmatic and got on with whatever had to be done. There is nothing else you can do. Crying and being miserable does not help anything; that has always been my reaction to things. I'm strong-minded, practical. I wore a beautiful backless dress the other night to an event, customised by my seamstress. You could never tell I'd had a mastectomy, and I was glad that I had not had the reconstruction and left my back intact. There are some things in this life you don't have any control over, and it's important to recognise that.

The New Account

I was very lucky when I had the opportunity to get the big account, Bloomberg, in 1987. I sometimes think if somebody else had got that account, perhaps they would not have done as much with it as I did, but because of my personality and my relentless focus on client service, I just ran with it.

As soon as I arrived at Spicer & Pegler, I realised that one of their small but lucrative accounts was Bloomberg. Bloomberg opened their first office outside the US in London in 1986. In 1987, they seconded Stuart Bell, one of Mike Bloomberg's close senior employees, to run their London office. A meeting was subsequently arranged between me and Stuart in October to assist him with his UK and US tax issues. That day in October was the day of the 1987 hurricane, when Michael Fish, the BBC's chief weatherman, told us all, 'Go to bed, there's no hurricane,' and by the morning we woke up to a devastated scene all over London. There were so many trees uprooted; it was like a nightmare! I remember that day very well, because I got up to go and meet Stuart Bell and there were no Underground trains running. It took me a long time to get to work, but I made it – and needless to say, Michael Fish never recovered from that error!

Stuart and I hit it off from the first time we met. At that time, Bloomberg was operating from a small office in Old Street at the edge of the City, and they didn't even have proper desks and chairs. We held his arrival meeting in the main room with all kinds of wires on the floor and I sat on top of a box which held IT equipment. Stuart was a charming person, charismatic, clever and friendly. He really appreciated the support I gave him and his team. I was very responsive and always willing to go the extra mile. Pretty soon I was involved very deeply in all of Bloomberg's UK operations, and as they expanded into Europe, I was there to support them one hundred per cent. After a couple of years, Bloomberg moved to new offices in Finsbury Square, right in the City of London, where they remained until late 2017, when they moved into their spectacular offices in Cannon Street. Over the years, they renovated and expanded their Finsbury Square offices, taking up more space and building a bridge between the two buildings they used. Their offices were always buzzing with energy, with an open-style kitchen welcoming visitors and employees with an amazing selection of food and drinks. You could also admire the huge, elaborate fish tanks, a very distinctive characteristic they had in every office, no matter how small or large.

London was the main headquarters for the Deloitte services provided to Bloomberg globally and everything was controlled from London, so it was a lot of work, primarily because of Bloomberg's incredibly rapid expansion. The company was growing about two thousand per cent every year. Their main offices were in New York, London, Frankfurt, Tokyo, Hong Kong, Singapore, Sydney and Sao Paulo. Every branch manager had to recruit new people, and they also had seconded managers in different parts of the world – so people from Hong Kong would be transferred to Tokyo, people from Australia would be transferred to Hong Kong, and Deloitte provided all the tax consulting and compliance services for all those employees moving around the world. For every one of these people, we had to contact Human Resources in New York, organise the payroll, decide how to pay them and structure their packages, deal with all their tax returns and accounting and all the bookkeeping for the companies they had all over the world. We did not provide audit services for their main entities nor the legal work – they had their own lawyers – but we did everything else. If they were thinking about opening an office in another city or another country, we would prepare a report for them about the pros and cons – tax implications, any repercussions for employees, the company's corporate tax status, VAT implications and all the information a company needed. The numbers were growing, and day-to-day it was about meeting the continued demand for more people going somewhere.

As I arrived at Spicers in the summer of 1987, the firm's leadership recruited David Major, a very successful City-based financial advisor. His task was to set up a separate, one hundred per cent-owned subsidiary of Spicers, the Spicer Financial Services Co (SFS). David's goal was to set up a one-stop shop which could advise firms and high-net-worth individuals on all aspects of their financial requirements: investments, pensions, legal and trusts, and of course taxes. He asked me to join him and have the group that I ran as part of the international personal tax component of SFS, which I accepted. I was very excited to be part of this new initiative, and before long, my department was the fastest-growing and most profitable part of SFS. David was a great boss who allowed me to thrive and fly. He trusted me to grow the business and was not hesitant when I told him that I had to travel to Asia to ensure that my clients were taken care of properly and to continue assisting them with their UK tax issues. This was the paramount differentiating factor for my practice. I generated a lot of new work, and my reputation grew within our firm, and in the market among our competitors and clients. The first time I went to Japan on my own in October 1989, my mum said to me, 'Aren't you scared to go on your own? It's such a far-away country.' My dad, who was more adventurous and loved travelling, was very impressed, saying to me that it was, 'So great to visit the Land of the Rising Sun.' I told them that I wasn't scared at all but very excited!

Just so you understand the type of work I was doing, let me explain briefly what it involved. If you are a US citizen living outside the US, you are taxable on your worldwide income and gains, and must file a US tax return as well as a tax return in the country you live in, for example the UK. If you are a UK taxpayer living outside the UK, you must pay taxes in the country you live and work. However, unlike the US, if you are considered a non-UK resident, then you will only pay UK tax on UK-sourced income. There is no need to report your worldwide income, so the tax filing is simpler! Expatriates are the taxpayers who live and work outside their home countries, and this was the area of tax expertise that I developed for myself.

When businesses were looking to send an executive from the UK to Japan, I advised them on both their UK and Japanese taxes, not just the UK tax. All the other big firms were providing advice on UK tax and referred their clients to their overseas colleagues. However, through constantly studying the foreign tax jurisdictions' tax regimes, travelling to those locations and working closely with my overseas colleagues, I was able to learn fast and become proficient in tax planning across many overseas locations where all the companies were seconding their senior executives. When I first moved to Spicers, I could only advise clients on UK and US taxes, but all their UK-based clients were opening offices all over the world – so I followed them, my knowledge expanded and I was able to provide my clients with a genuinely unique proposition.

For two years since joining Spicers, my experience in international tax planning expanded to cover all of Asia, Europe and North America. All the major law firms, merchant banks and real estate companies were growing their overseas presence and needed reliable UK executives as well as junior employees to run their overseas offices. The senior executives or partners ran the offices while the junior employees were learning and developing their skills in conjunction with local hires. These youngsters would later move to other locations as senior employees. Eventually, they would return to London, New York or wherever they originally came from, to lead those companies or firms, or become part of the companies' leadership teams. This enabled me to forge strong and lifelong contacts, which allowed me to take my career from strength to strength.

In any case, wherever I went, I always connected with my colleagues in the local offices and met with my clients, most of whom I knew from London. In those days we didn't have the technology to take notes on our iPads or iPhones. Instead, I used to take notes by hand, which I faxed back to London, and my secretary would type them up and fax them back for me to review. I was always busy, so I could only work on and review my notes while I was on the move, either in cars going from the hotels to the airports or vice versa while travelling between locations, always working and making the to-do lists so my team would deliver on the action points. These trips always generated a lot of work every time and enabled me to forge strong ongoing relationships. I always delivered on the promises I made! I carried our latest booklets and newsflashes, and updates on tax-efficient investments which my colleagues in the investment advisory part of our firm prepared specifically for my use. All the UK expatriates were very interested to find out where they could invest their money, and most of them bought UK houses which they rented out so they didn't feel they were out of the UK housing market.

In the old days, I would go to Asia for ten days – two weeks would have been too much, but because I tended to stay for ten days it meant I was always there for at least one weekend. I preferred being in Hong Kong rather than Tokyo because in Tokyo

Ellie's family in 1959; Ellie is five years old

Ellie in 1972, before coming to London to study

1975, LSE weekend retreat

1976, CASS Business School, London: Ellie, Egly, Metin and other students

Ellie and Philip, June 11, 1978: their wedding day in Aradippou

1980, Ellie with Maria in Houston, Texas

July 1983, Ellie with Nicolas in The Bahamas

1983, Maria and Nicolas at home in Houston, Texas

1983, Ellie, Philip, Maria and Nicolas at home in Houston, Texas

there were always more restrictions on what I could do. Hong Kong had an expatriate community with a lot of people coming in and out, so I always felt like I had more options. On Saturdays, if the weather was nice, I would go for a run and then spend all day by the pool, catching up on my most recent meetings and writing notes in preparation for the following week. Sometimes I would have a massage at the hotel spa, and then in the evening I would always try to arrange dinner with a client or colleague, or I would watch a movie. It felt strange, sometimes, doing that – once I found myself in Tokyo among all these Japanese people watching *Jurassic Park*!

At the time, I was one of the few professionals in the UK making these regular trips in Asia and all over the world. It was always exciting, but it was very lonely, sometimes, because I travelled from city to city, meeting so many clients from each firm. Sometimes I felt like an early cowboy pushing forward on new frontiers, and sometimes it felt as if I had a doctor's surgery, meeting so many people back-to-back! It was a strange life sometimes – ten days on the road, meetings, breakfasts, lunches and dinners every day. I had to be very disciplined and go to the gym every day because there was so much food, and opportunities to eat and drink all the time. Sometimes I weighed a little more than I do now, but never too much, because I was very careful and relentless with my gym-going and running. Sometimes it was just easier to get room service, but I tried to stop myself from doing that all the time. I would have to tell myself, 'I am not going to have room service today. I'll go downstairs and eat in the restaurant.'

Mergers and Acquisitions

In 1990, the financial world was badly shaken by the Big Bang. In previous years, there had been a relaxation to the bank regulatory regime and the banks had grown and grown. Everyone expected the growth to continue, but it did not, so a lot of companies were caught unawares, having invested heavily in new people and new offices. At that time, our firm was called Spicer & Oppenheim because we had entered a new global network of accounting firms. In 1990, our Spicer & Oppenheim US firm overextended itself, having invested in new offices while still leasing their existing office space. When the good times turned sour, they couldn't absorb all the costs and went under. As the largest firm of the global network, it had a huge impact on the rest of the group. The global network of Spicer & Oppenheim was broken, and talks started in the UK with Touche Ross & Co, one of the Big Eight firms at that time, to discuss a potential merger.

After the Big Bang, there was a lot of consolidation among the Big Eight firms. Ernst & Whinney merged with Arthur Young and became Ernst & Young. Peat Marwick merged with Klynveld Main Goerdeler to become KPMG. Deloitte Haskins & Sells merged with Touche Ross everywhere in the world, apart from the UK, due to Deloitte's UK leadership, who opted to join Coopers & Lybrand, and they were called Coopers & Lybrand Deloitte. Following all these mergers and the professional firms' consolidation, Price Waterhouse merged with Coopers & Lybrand Deloitte and became PWC. Once PWC was created, most of the Deloitte partners in the UK were either fired or not given any senior positions, and most of them left. The PWC merger was the least successful for several years because the two firms operated separately and behaved as two firms, hence all the expected synergies did not materialise for a long time.

After all these mergers, the new Big Five firms were PWC, KPMG, E&Y, Arthur Andersen and Deloitte & Touche, which was called Deloitte & Touche (D&T) everywhere in the world apart from the UK, where the original name of Touche Ross continued for five years until the global firm bought the Deloitte name in the UK from PWC. During this upheaval, the UK Touche Ross firm could not cope with the huge amount of referral work they were receiving from the US and other overseas firms, so they were looking to take over a respectable UK firm. It was at that time that Spicer & Oppenheim was facing problems due to its global network collapse. The timing was perfect! Touche Ross took over Spicer & Oppenheim in the UK, and some of the Spicer & Oppenheim firms around the world also joined, including Hong Kong, Australia, Belgium and Switzerland, in late 1990. The other firms joined another global network which was much smaller than ours.

Touche Ross was a much bigger firm than Spicer & Oppenheim and all their departments were larger than ours. They had about fifty people in their expatriate tax department (my department-to-be!), whereas in my department at Spicer & Oppenheim there were only five. However, my team was performing more efficiently and strategically than theirs. At the time, the partner in charge of that department, Peter Shawyer, was somewhat unhelpful because he didn't know me very well and didn't appreciate the kind of work we did. He was aware of my reputation for travelling all over the world, and thought I was just travelling for the sake of it! He was always checking me out, even though I was not part of his department, and we were in different buildings – I was still reporting to David Major and we were operating as SFS-Touche Ross from the original Spicer & Oppenheim offices in the City. At the same time, David Major was not willing to allow me to move departments and join the bigger Touche Ross expatriate tax team, because I was the most profitable part of his operation, but he was getting all the credit as the only partner in SFS. Because of that, he didn't want to let me go and wasn't actively supporting me to enter the process to be considered for partner promotion, so I found myself in a quandary.

I said to Philip, 'The only way to escape this situation is to take the plunge and go to Peter Shawyer, who doesn't particularly like me, because he thinks I am not working hard and I am always travelling – but when he realises what I do, as the professional that he is, I am sure he will understand. David will not do anything, since he continues to benefit from the revenue I generate. I must do something!'

I decided to act, and I talked in confidence to a member of Peter's team. Following that, they asked me to move with them overnight. David was very upset, but I said, 'What can I do? He's the big boss and he's asked me to join his group!'

In 1991 I arrived at Hill House, where the Touche Ross expatriate tax team was based. It was obvious I was far ahead of everybody there. When I worked at the Crutched Friars building, Peter kept telling me that I was taking all the work coming to the UK from several overseas offices (not the large multinational contracts that Deloitte in the US primarily controlled from the US). I said, 'Listen, I am the best here, so when I talk to the people from overseas and they get to know me, they want me to be on their accounts! It's not my fault – tell your people to get over it and try and provide a better client service.' When I explained to him what I was doing, and the type of services I provided to my clients, he could see I was doing something totally different; it was not just inbound work but more outbound work, covering the tax planning for both the home country and the host country.

During my overseas trips, I visited my clients with local colleagues who didn't have any relationships locally, but due to my introductions, they became involved, so both the clients and my colleagues were very happy with me. I had annual visits to key financial centres in Asia, including Tokyo, Hong Kong, Singapore, Sydney, Melbourne, and when China opened up in the early 1990s, I added Beijing and Shanghai. Later, I added Delhi, Mumbai and Seoul. Those were hard years because I visited so many clients, and many individuals per client. Bloomberg was always my priority, and over the years, when the global firm introduced the concept of one partner being globally responsible for all the services the firm provided to our clients, I was appointed as the Global Lead Client Service Partner for Bloomberg (GLCSP). I had so many deep relationships across the Deloitte firms and all my clients. All the senior partners of the law firms and the CEOs of the financial institutions were very happy with my visits. I was invited to join them and their spouses for dinner at restaurants, at social events or in their homes, and I felt so welcome. Peter realised quickly that I was very hard-working and successful. I offered more to my clients than his team, so he realised that my work was more effective and more profitable! After that, things were easier between the two of us, and I really began to fly.

When Eastern Europe opened up in 1992, I embraced it with enthusiasm. By that time, I had been promoted from senior manager to principal, the grade below partner. At the firm, it was standard practice for one to do a minimum of two years in the principal role and then move on to be considered for the equity partner role. By that time, Peter Shawyer had become my mentor, and he felt that if I were involved in a new initiative, it would help my case to be promoted to partner, so I was sent to Warsaw in Poland to set up their tax department. Before 1992, Eastern Europe was still under the communist regime, so nobody was paying taxes, and they didn't even have a tax regime. My first trip was in late February just after we'd moved into our current family house in Eversley Crescent. The house was lovely, with a much bigger garden, but as soon as we moved, and before we established a routine and got used to the new house, I had to go to Poland. I used to fly late on Sunday and return with the last flight on Friday. This routine continued for many months.

In those days the best hotel to stay in Warsaw was the Marriott, where all the expatriates from the UK, the US and elsewhere stayed. The hotel had a great bakery, which had the most amazing cinnamon bread I had ever tasted. Everyone in our family loves cinnamon, so every week I placed my order for three loaves of cinnamon bread because Philip and the children were expecting them. If I didn't order them in advance, there was no chance I would be able to find them by Friday afternoon!

Spending so much time in Warsaw was an eye-opener. All the staff members of Deloitte Warsaw were very nice and worked hard, but due to the oppressive regime they had lived through for so long, they had some strange phobias. For example, they always wanted the office doors in their rooms to be closed so no one could see what they were doing. Since we were promoting the concept of an open-door policy, we used to go around and open all the doors by mid-morning, but by lunchtime, they were closed again! It took a long time for them to feel at ease. I made some great friends in the tax department, in particular Andrei, the tax partner, and Anna, a lovely manager whom I trained to get to senior manager. I remember that, during one of my visits, she insisted that I go for dinner with her so that I would meet her husband and young son. It was a cold and icy day, and it had snowed heavily the night before, but her husband picked me up by car and we set off for their house. Their house was at least two hours away from the centre of Warsaw and the driving conditions were bad. I was very scared and thought we would never make it alive to their house. But we did, and we had a great dinner. She also gave me some goodies to take home, mushrooms and other vegetables in vinegar, their speciality. Philip was very pleased with them.

In 1992, Warsaw was very dark and depressing. All the buildings were grey concrete, very representative of the Soviet architectural style. When the weather opened up in late spring, it was much better, and I even managed to visit Kraków, a beautiful town full of lovely buildings and an amazing castle. I took the bullet train on my own to visit it on a weekday, which fell on a public holiday. I wasn't afraid; I felt very safe. I found some American tourists in Kraków, and we saw the local sights together.

Poland was an amazing experience – it was a whole new country, new regime and new way of thinking. I wrote tax newsflashes and articles about the new regime which were published throughout the tax community. I also presented at many internal and external client conferences on the new tax changes in Eastern and Central Europe. I worked in the Czech Republic, Russia, Hungary, and all the Eastern and Central European countries. Due to my exposure at conferences as a speaker and the fact that I was becoming much more of an authority, people knew Ellie Patsalos. For example, when there was talk about David Beckham moving to Spain, I gave an interview to the *Daily Telegraph* about tax planning and what happens when a UK resident goes overseas to live and work. I also gave an interview to the CNN weekend programme about UK expatriates living in Singapore, and how they were taxed on their UK and offshore investments.

In those days, I was rarely at home, because I was travelling all the time. When the kids were younger, I used to lay out their outfits for every day of the week before I left, because Philip had no colour coordination whatsoever! I loved travelling, but I also loved the feeling of coming home.

The Ellie Effect

On the first of June 1995, I became an equity partner. It was very tough to get onto the partner assessment course. The senior leadership had to approve the potential partners and a list was prepared, so the more partners you knew, and who liked you, the better! I had lunch with one of the senior partners from Spicer & Oppenheim, who knew me very well, so he was selected to have a frank discussion with me before I was added to the potential partner list.

He said, 'Ellie, you're very good, but you know, your English is not all that great.'

I said, 'What do you mean, it's not all that great? My English is better than some British people's, because outside the UK we were taught proper grammar and spelling. I have written articles and advisory letters, so don't tell me my English is not good!'

He said, 'OK, but the way you dress, you know, it's quite modern...'

I always loved clothes, so I had a very distinctive dress sense; once you met me you never forgot me. I always bought lovely clothes, of the type that were fashionable at the time – mini-skirts, shoulder pads and my hair permed – it was all very *Dynasty*.

I said, 'That's who I am. If you don't like it, I'm out of here. I have so many offers; I could go to someone else who will value me the way I am! Clients love me; maybe not everybody, but most people appreciate me. And my revenues are much higher than what a senior partner delivers to the firm. This is my answer; I will not change for anyone.'

The following day they said to me, 'Ellie, we love you just the way you are, and you're not going anywhere; you're going to be a partner here at Touche Ross.'

The partner assessment course was one of the most dramatic experiences in my professional life. It took place in January 1995 and was very tough, but I managed to make it! It was a nightmare the way we were pushed to the limit, having to be involved in multiple tasks at the same time. I went to the course feeling terrible, with a bad cold and feeling very sad, having lost Philip's dad on 31st December 1994. He was always in very good health. He developed a hernia and whilst it was being investigated, the doctor also diagnosed that he had an aortic aneurysm, so he had to have an operation to remove it. The four-hour operation went well, he woke up and chatted to the family, including the kids, and all was fine. However, the following day he developed a chest infection, and due to his lifelong twenty-cigarettes-per-day smoking habit, he went into a coma and never recovered. We were all very shocked by his sudden unexpected death.

There was a funny moment in my partner assessment course. It was a three-day event, and as I said, at the time I had a very bad cold and I was really feeling unwell. The head of HR, Paul Williams, who was also leading the assessment course, asked us a question with all of us sitting around the room. He said, 'One of the problems we have as a client service firm is that we can serve our clients in the UK, New York, Canada and the Netherlands very well because we have big practices in these countries, but the challenge we face is when we go to a small office in Buenos Aires, Sao Paulo or Vietnam. How can you get the Deloitte colleagues to give to our client's small operation in their country the same kind of service that they get, and they expect from us, because of their experience in, say, London?'

I said to him, 'For my clients, it's the Ellie effect.'

He said, 'What do you mean?'

I said, 'I go to these offices every year, so we see eye to eye. I say to them, "I will treat you well and pay you good rates, and you will give my client an excellent service. And if you don't, I will be coming back next year, so don't think you're getting rid of me."' It was just so funny the way I said it with conviction and very seriously that everyone burst into laughter! But that's exactly how it worked. Our US colleagues were dealing with global clients, but they never travelled overseas. They were so reluctant to go to these countries where their clients were based, so they never developed the strong relationships that I had. When you have that personal rapport, and you look them in the eye, they do not let you down, because they know you. At the end of the partner assessment course Paul mentioned it again – he was making a final speech to all of us and outlined some of the highlights and funny elements of the three-day course, and he talked about the Ellie effect!

Early in my life as a tax partner, one of our practices was to have tables ranking each partner in the tax practice for the amounts of bills rendered, cash targets and revenues coming in. Those tables were circulated amongst all the partners to see – there were about forty tax partners in total, women and men – and I was always at the very top of the tables. Accounting firms are made up of different service areas – Audit, Tax, Consulting, Corporate Finance, and Mergers & Acquisitions (M&A). I was part of the tax department, and so it was not only selling services that was important, but cash collection was vital! We billed quarterly in those days, and you had to make sure that you collected the money. Every partner's cash target was based on the amount of bills they issued. Some partners did not pay as much attention as they should to either billing or collection. They felt that they had done their part and were not always efficient in executing the billing and cash collection part of the business, which in my view was fundamental. I was always very commercial, very aware of money. I told everyone that trained under me, 'Every time I come to the office and I turn the lights on, it costs us millions! When we get a new client, we must deliver services. As a firm, we pay you for the work done and we, in return, need to get the revenues, so we must bill for our services, otherwise no revenue comes in!' If a partner missed their cash target, then they would suffer financially so that their quarterly distribution was deferred for three more months. Once those tables were circulated among the partners, I would always try to help the partners at the bottom of the league. I would meet with them and ask them, 'What's wrong? When do you bill? Why aren't you billing them? Why don't you call them and say, "You need to pay us?"?' I would tell them, 'I think if you are respected and have a good relationship with your clients, you can be open with them and tell them that if they don't pay us on time you will be financially adversely affected.' This process enabled me to get a very good reputation among the other partners. I was so successful that management asked me to mentor tax partners who never billed or collected revenues on time.

I strongly believe that clients want to deal with a company that is financially successful. If you do not bill and collect on time, it looks like something is wrong. You cannot go ahead and borrow from the bank to fund services to clients, so I was always very upfront with my clients. In the outside world, nobody gets five months' credit – the bank would never give you one month's credit, let alone five months. Mentioning fees is not embarrassing. If I do the work, I want to be paid! Sometimes the money from our clients was just caught up in the internal system, even if the invoice was approved, and sometimes the company did delay paying bills on a regular basis, so one had to act! Deloitte had a team in each service line that was dedicated to monitoring the outstanding bills and contacting the accounts departments of our clients to find out the status of our bills, so we were involved directly after the team had tried already!

In 1995, when I made partner, Bloomberg was my number-one client, but I also had law firms, merchant banks and so many other clients. I was at the height of my career, and then, in 1996, the icing on the cake came. I took over the HSBC account, which was known as Hong Kong Shanghai Banking Corporation at the time, and it was a very competitive bid. Because Bloomberg was blossoming, I was travelling all over the world visiting their offices. As HSBC was to become a global client also, for initially a three-year contract for their expatriate population, I would thus be able to combine visiting the Bloomberg businesses and meeting all the HSBC expatriates, the local senior leadership and all other clients and contacts I had developed. I was the Global Lead Tax Partner with Peter Shawyer as the Advisory Partner on the HSBC account, supported by a strong team in the UK and globally. It started with a three-year contract, then it was extended to five years and from there it grew, so by 2012, I had been the Global Lead Client Partner for sixteen years. The global revenues were very high, and HSBC was one of the top five global financial services accounts.

During my time as Global Lead Client Service Partner (GLCSP) for HSBC, I have known four chairmen and three CEOs. I got along with all of them, even if they didn't always get along with each other! I am still friends with all of them, and one former CEO, whom I see regularly, attended my son Nicolas's wedding in Cyprus. I travelled all over the world in Europe, Asia, Canada, the US and finally Latin America. I was in such a strong position those days that I knew everybody's role, and for some of them, I knew where they were headed before they knew themselves. HSBC had an elite programme called International Managers (IMs), and they were the top managers of the global bank. They were hired specifically for this prestigious programme and they committed to moving around the world. If the bank asked them to move, usually every two years, they would move, no questions asked! In return, HSBC would pay them very well, provide an excellent pension and take care of everything: the move, storage in the home country, children's education, boarding schools, housing, they took care of it all. I would go and see them in Hong Kong and Sao Paulo, and then in Australia, and then in Tokyo, Mumbai, Singapore, all over the world, because they were International Managers and they were constantly on the move! The IMs had very senior roles; they were the senior executives of the bank. For example, if an IM moved from Japan to India as the country's CEO, my Indian colleagues wanted to meet the new CEO, so I arranged for them to meet. I went to India and arranged for Deloitte to see the new CEO, arranged meetings with the various functional leaders, e.g. in Risk and Compliance, Human Capital, Mergers & Acquisitions (M&A), Tax, Strategy, Technology and so on, so the various Deloitte partners who specialised in these areas would forge relationships and provide services to them. Some of these senior leaders or IMs would then move to Sao Paulo, and I would go to Sao Paulo and do the same. I arranged meetings with everyone, basically; Deloitte colleagues knew that, because they experienced it in practice. That was very powerful for us, to be able to have meetings with these senior leaders. During my regular visits, in addition to meetings in the office, I would also meet them for breakfast, dinner or lunch in their private dining rooms, in their offices or in restaurants. Spouses accompanied us and therefore I became close to them too. Everyone knew that I was close to these senior executives, and they treated me with respect. Every year there was more and more travelling, seeing more and more clients.

Gaining HSBC as a new client, with me as the lead partner on the account, was a real turning point for me! As the years progressed, the people I knew as my clients progressed themselves within the bank and became senior executives. Deloitte provided services to different industries, but financial services was by far the biggest global industry because it comprised the banks, all the financial institutions, insurance companies, hedge funds, private equity and so on. In the early days HSBC was a small account, but because the executives we looked after progressed within the bank, opportunities grew with them, and I was very well placed because I knew everyone. All the people I helped on a personal basis, who had gone to Japan, Hong Kong, Australia or Europe, were promoted themselves, and therefore they had more budgets and needed more services.

So that's how it all started. I became the lead partner globally for HSBC for all the services that Deloitte provided, and that meant that I travelled even more than before. Before, I was travelling for Bloomberg and all the law firms and merchant banks, and now I was also travelling for HSBC, and I needed to continue to grow the account and thereby progress within Deloitte. I started helping other partners, both in the UK and overseas, to sell more services to HSBC, for example, in Risk and Advisory, Compliance, Cost Cutting, Technology and M&A, among others. All the big global banks had operations in the US, so if they didn't properly adhere to all the regulations that the US imposed on them in order for them to continue dealing in US dollars and maintaining a presence in the US, they were in deep trouble and had to rectify their processes.

I was renowned throughout the global Deloitte firm for always providing extra service to my clients. Once I got a client, I never lost them. I think it came back to that passion for providing an excellent service. It started when I was in Aradippou with my dad, telling his customers, 'I don't have what you need now, but I'll bring it to you.' I always did deliver on our promise! That commitment of always providing a great service, that ethos of fulfilling your promise, started for me very early on. When I was building up my career, I had never thought about a management position because my real love was client service. Generating revenues and providing a consistently excellent service to my clients was my priority. In those days, however, the only way you could progress was through a management role, but gradually they realised that client service was the most powerful. Suddenly it was this big, fashionable thing – developing client relationships and cross-selling – and I had been doing it for years as a junior manager!

Really, keeping clients happy is very simple. They know that you cannot do everything right, sometimes things will not go according to plan, but as long as you promise them that you will take care of the problem and you do on a timely basis, then it's fine. No matter how presentable I was and the first good impression I made, if I didn't have substance, if I didn't deliver, then I wouldn't have kept the clients for too long. It's the constant communication, I kept telling my people. Communication is the key thing. Silence is a killer. Nobody wants to wonder whether you received their email or letter. Just say, 'I've got it, I'll get back to you.' That's all they need, but some people don't get it. Furthermore, some professionals prefer to email rather than pick up the phone and speak to their client or arrange to meet them. But I used to say to them, get on the phone, sort it out and have a meeting. Because every time you go to a meeting, you get new business. There's no way you'll end a face-to-face meeting without any follow-up, which translates to more work. That's how it is! You talk to your clients about new developments, new challenges, their future plans for expansion, and that's where the opportunities are.

New Business

One Friday night, Philip and I were having dinner in London with the CEO of HSBC and his wife. He asked me, 'Has the CEO of HSBC in the US called you?' I said, 'No,' and he said, 'Call him, because they have a big IRS audit and Deloitte can help. I think he already called PWC, and we agreed that he was also going to call you, so I suggest you call him and say that your CEO asked you to call.'

Consequently, I called the CEO of HSBC US over the weekend, and he called me back and explained what they were looking for. I briefed my Deloitte team in New York, we went to see him and we got the work. This was one of the biggest projects we had ever undertaken for HSBC. It was a huge project, with work carried out in the US, the UK, Hong Kong and Dubai. In the UK we rented offices in Canary Wharf, in one of the big warehouses which was empty at the time, and we had over a thousand Deloitte people working there together with HSBC employees. Because we did not have enough people available straight away to go and do this work, we subcontracted with another company that provided people, plus our own specialists and HSBC.

As the Global Lead Client Service Partner for the account, I was known all over our global network with the excellent reputation that the client trusted me and turned to me when they needed a trustworthy firm to assist them. On the basis that

I was the one who had made the introduction to the US team, I continued to be involved in this project, which was very positive for me. We had a similar situation a few years earlier with Barclays. For example, in Deloitte Mexico, if they had a team that was not fully utilised, they were sent to New York, or similarly if there were teams in Continental Europe with capacity, they came to London to assist the local team, get training on the job for such big projects and take the experience back to their home countries. All these professionals were part of the Global Financial Services Industry (GFSI).

I was appointed as a member of the board and of the executive of GFSI and as the Global Head of Financial Services Tax in late 2007. I was also a member of the Global Tax Executive. I had my own global FSI tax network. I appointed regional leaders: one in Europe, the Middle East and Africa (EMEA), one in the Americas, and one in the Asia Pacific. We had monthly calls, which all the top FSI tax partners who serviced our top thirty Global FSI clients participated in. The purpose of these calls was to ensure that everyone was aware of the latest technical developments, which global projects had been sold to clients and which ones could be relevant for other global clients with similar footprints. A team from a particular global account presented an update on that account and materials were shared amongst the teams; of course, nothing confidential that couldn't be shared. Every year, with the assistance of my small team and the goodwill of my fellow FS tax partners, we prepared a Tax Thought Leadership Publication, and the contents were used as our key talking and presentational pieces for our various internal and client conferences. We had one FSI Client Tax Conference in New York in March, one in an Asian financial centre in late April, and another in Europe, the Middle East and Africa (EMEA) in late June. These were very successful and were attended by many of our FSI clients. I held specific internal FSI tax sessions and breakfast meetings for all the Deloitte attendees from all over the world to prepare us for the client meetings ahead of us. My predecessor never managed to get the buy-in or had the discipline to produce a publication for four years and I had one published every year! The Global FSI team assisted financially in its preparation and distribution globally which helped. These roles, although prestigious, didn't come with much budget facilities! I held this role for seven years until I retired, and alas, my successor did not do much; he stopped all these touchpoints and has now been replaced with one of the UK tax partners who was the head of EMEA during my service.

As a senior partner on key accounts, my motto has always been to assist other partners from other service lines to get in front of my clients, which benefits the clients, the partners and the firm as a whole! I feel that is the best behaviour for a partner, because some partners were very protective of their clients. I was always very open, and my attitude was, 'Come on in! The more we sell, the more everybody benefits.' I asked my colleagues to provide me with a short description of the product or new idea they were trying to promote so I could pass it by my contacts, and if we felt it would benefit them, then a meeting was set up to introduce the idea. Clients always wanted to hear the latest ideas in the marketplace, so they were willing to meet with the specialists. Also, the reputation of Deloitte rises because the clients appreciate the kind of talent you have everywhere, not just in the UK. In London and New York, it is easy to find good talent, but when you go to Argentina, Iceland, Vietnam or Africa it was more of a problem, because it became more challenging to provide consistent service everywhere. When the clients are in a small country and they are small themselves, they want great support locally, not just from the centre. A lot of firms lack that local support, and we were no exception. From my perspective, I was frustrated about our lack of a strong FSI presence in Asia, and I was very vocal about it at the board meetings. Everyone knew when I started complaining about the lack of investment in Asia, it was like, 'Here we go again...', but it was very important to my HSBC relationship. Apart from London, they were strongest in Hong Kong and Shanghai, and we did not have a great FSI team there at the time compared to our competitors, PWC. The global firm agreed with me, but it was quite difficult to implement our strategy and obtain good talent from our existing teams.

Every function had a leader, the Head of Tax, Head of Consulting, Head of Audit, Head of Corporate Finance and M&A. Each function had a board in each country and globally, there was a Global Board. Since I was part of the tax group, and as Global Head of FSI Tax, I had a seat on the Global Tax Executive. That group determined the policy and implementation of all the strategies for global tax. We had representations from the top ten countries and some of the global service lines such as IT, Human Capital and from the industries, only the FSI leader was included and that was me. Each service line had client conferences each year depending on the area concerned, as well as internal conferences for training and development purposes. That was how we connected with a lot of colleagues and clients. In the FSI world, we had special workshops for all the teams across different service lines and sectors to learn about the latest developments from each other. We presented some of the most successful global projects in certain accounts, and some of the achievements on those accounts, so everyone would be aware of the most up-to-date developments that could be relevant to their clients and try to cross-reference. Those were very important meetings.

Every year we had a Global Financial Services Client conference by strict invitation only. The financial services industry was the most important industry in Deloitte, and the most successful. During the first year as the GLCSP for HSBC, I could invite someone from HSBC to attend with their spouse. Therefore, I invited the CEO of the HSBC UK Retail Bank and his wife, and Philip also joined me. My guest was a Canadian who was seconded to the UK, and he was the head of the UK Retail Bank. Everything was paid for, and all they had to pay was their airfares to get there. Such clients participated or presented during the conference. We had a fantastic time. That was the first time I could invite a client, as you had to have a certain type of client, but after that first year, I invited someone from HSBC every year. Since I only invited the top leaders, they wanted me to also be involved with the presentations at the event. Jack Ribeiro, the GFSI leader, asked me to make the introductions for all the speakers, starting with the introduction of the morning speakers, and later it included all the speakers for the entire day, which was quite hard work, but it was good to be on stage and for everyone to know me! I had beautiful outfits for the day events as well as for the evening events, including the glamorous black-tie dinners! Those conferences were always held in amazing hotels and beautiful cities such as Venice, Vienna, Paris, Rome, Prague, Athens, Madrid, Lisbon, Berlin, Hong Kong, Istanbul and Singapore. In the last five or so years, I stopped attending the expatriate tax conferences since I just couldn't be everywhere. Younger partners took over these client meetings. When you are a partner at a Big Four firm, and you are a senior partner with lots of responsibilities, you are not always around, you are travelling practically every week. There are so many demands on your time.

On the Board

During the 1990s, there were not many female partners. There were about sixteen, and most of them dressed like men because they wanted to conform to what the 'elders' required and expected, or what they thought the clients wanted. This was especially true for the women who worked in the audit practice, who had to deal with CFOs and boards entirely made up of older men. As I was in tax, I was mainly dealing with HR and tax departments around the world, and they often had a different perspective. The people I worked with on a day-to-day basis were likely to be younger.

I never changed how I dressed or presented myself. In those days, we had 'dress-down Fridays', where the men wore chinos, and the women wore more casual clothes and flat shoes. Most of our clients had the same policy, but I was never into it – I never changed my style! During one of our annual partner conferences, John Connolly, the CEO at the time, gave a prize for the 'Best Dressed-Down Man and Woman of the Year'. The man was selected for his unusual dressed-down style, but for the woman, he chose me for not adhering at all to the new policy! I was told about this beforehand, so for that evening I wore a long, glamorous gold gown. He told everyone that Deloitte had introduced a 'dress-down' policy, but, as he said, 'Ellie does not listen to anyone; she continues to dress glamorously. This is how Ellie dresses – like the

Oscars!' I had my speech prepared, and I thanked my parents, my teacher, my husband and children, everyone – like they do at the Oscars, getting emotional and everything – and then I said, 'John, to continue to maintain the quality and style of my wardrobe, I need an allowance. And since I work in the expatriate tax area, it must be grossed up – so shall we say ten thousand pounds a year to start with?' Everyone in the audience laughed, including John!

During that time everybody knew me because of my reputation as a successful client service partner for key accounts, and for my extravagant style of dress and my outgoing personality, so I had a lot of support. All the partners knew me, and all the firm's senior people were aware of Ellie – I was 'the Ellie' to them. At every conference we attended, people always said they were looking forward to seeing what I was wearing! But all of this means nothing if you don't have substance. What really matters is hard work, excellent client service and revenues coming in.

We created a board position specifically for women because we realised that the firm was so male-dominated there was no way that a woman had a fair chance of election. In addition to the board positions for each function, participation from the firm's executive, the regions and Switzerland (which became part of the UK firm), we created two more board positions for women, one for the London office and one for the regions. We became like the UK Parliament, where you elect MPs from different parts of the country to represent different constituencies.

One day David Cruickshank, the firm's chairman and a senior tax partner (previously Head of UK Tax), called me and said, 'Ellie, I think you should run for the board. I have received many nominations from partners who would like to see you on the board, and I fully support it.'

David was a very good friend of mine. He was a junior partner in tax before I made partner, and I remember the Head of Tax at the time, my mentor Peter Shawyer, telling me, 'David is going to go far in our firm, he's so smart.' He became Head of Tax after Peter and now he was asking me to run for the board.

I said, 'David, I'm so busy! I am the Global LCSP for Bloomberg and HSBC, I am the Global Head of FSI Tax, I am on the Global Board and Global Executive for GFSI, on the Global Tax Executive – plus all the other clients I have and the other day-to-day responsibilities! How can I also take on this role?'

He said, 'Ellie, you can do it. It will not take a lot of your time, it's only monthly, and I believe we would benefit from having you on the board. People respect you.'

I was very reluctant, but eventually, after discussing it with Philip and some of my colleagues, I said, why not? I would give it a try. I was delighted when I was elected with a huge majority, and in fact, I served the maximum three terms allowed (two years per term, so six years in total). I loved it! When you are on the board, you have access to all the firm's issues, and you know everything that is going on in the firm. It elevated me to a new dimension and provided me with a very rewarding experience. We also had contact with the Global Deloitte Board and Global CEO/chairman.

However, during that time, I realised having one woman on the board wasn't very effective. You need at least two, ideally more. If you have one woman, no matter how senior she is, she tends to be intimidated by the men. If you have two, you connect, and if you have three, you have a quorum. David Cruickshank, who was the chairman throughout my tenure as a board member, used to say what a difference it made to have more than one female member on the board! Women bring a very different perspective, which comes naturally and makes the debate and decision-making richer. When I retired from Deloitte and he finished his full tenure as UK chairman, he was elected as chairman of the Global Board, and at that time he said to me, 'It's so amazing, you see that women look at things from a different angle. It's not a right or wrong angle, just a different angle, and the debate changes. You end up arriving in a better position, a better situation than before,' and I agreed with him.

John Connolly set up a Women's Leadership Committee. There were four very senior partners: me; Margaret Ewing, who was already a vice-chairman; Sharon Thorne, who was head of audit in the regions; and Heather Hancock, a partner in consulting. In addition to supporting and mentoring the female staff members and female partners, we also supported Emma Codd, who was the head of the firm's Women's Network. Emma was a partner in the M&A practice and before I retired, she was promoted to head of HR, a role that she still held very successfully until recently! While I was on the board, we worked on improving the women's initiatives, such as part-time working, maternity leave and all the softer things that took much longer to implement. We had more women on the board and more help to champion and push these new initiatives forward. We realised that we lost a lot of our female employees at senior manager levels when they would leave to have their first baby and not come back, and we knew that we had to make it easier for them to return. It was particularly difficult for audit and consulting employees coming back from maternity leave because they would have been more likely to work on audits or consulting projects for companies based outside London, and you could not have a new mother back from maternity leave stuck for a week or more all over the country! We allowed these women to work in different roles, not reducing their status but giving them different types of jobs so that they would not have to be away from home. We would facilitate their going home early, to feed the kids, bathe them and put them to bed, and they could then log on later to catch up on anything urgent that had to be taken care of. We had meetings to discuss issues facing partners, directors or senior managers who were back from maternity leave. These initiatives were very much welcomed.

During that period, we had a few acquisitions; it was a new experience for me to be involved in M&A transactions for the firm. We had urgent weekend calls where we received updates and information, and we voted on whether to proceed or not. Another interesting experience from my board years was when we introduced non-executive directors (NEDs). We added three NEDs to the board because although it was customary for the corporates, it was not so typical for professional firms like ours. However, since it was seen as best practice, Deloitte embraced it. We appointed three NEDs, a woman and two men who were experienced and well respected in their fields of expertise.

Going back to those days, some of the male partners did not like it when women left at 6pm or could not attend client events in the evening, and they would make sarcastic comments. Our CEO had traditional notions. Like a lot of the older generation, he didn't support the idea of working from home. We discussed this at length and argued with him, but even though the policy was changed to facilitate part-time working when appropriate, his heart wasn't in it. I think he tried to understand it and sometimes he paid lip service to it, but he did not really believe in it. It was the same with partners taking sabbaticals. After ten years, you could take a sabbatical of four, six or eight weeks, and his attitude was that, 'Only wimps take sabbaticals.' Who would take a sabbatical after hearing that? It was only after our new CEO, David Sproul, took over that these policies really became entrenched in our day-to-day practice.

We encouraged the women to be more vocal and put themselves forward for board positions in their service lines or push for Lead Client Service Partner (LCSP) positions. As a result, some changes were made to our policies, but it was still hard for the women to be outspoken and not be intimidated. If you were a mother, travelling could be another challenge. I was travelling all the time, but I had Philip and his parents looking after the kids. A lot of women did not have that support. They had nannies that cost a lot of money, but because they were well compensated, it was often the only way around it. Women must be strong and not always feel guilty; that's how life is. You must make hard decisions and, once these decisions are taken, you must look forward! I always said to the girls that I mentored and who had children, 'Don't look back and feel guilty. If you go back to work, you feel guilty; if you stay home, you feel unhappy. You must decide what you want and go for it, otherwise you have a whole life of guilt. Your mental state goes downhill, and nobody benefits. What's the point?'

As mentioned earlier, the Women's Leadership Committee did a lot of good work over those years. I believe that we set up the foundation for all the positive changes introduced subsequently.

Nowadays the technology is such that you can work remotely very successfully. In those days, you did not have computers or the ability to work from home and be connected. Now, everybody has a secure connection from home to the office, and they just log on and there it is. Of course, you still need to be in the office for personal day-to-day interaction, but it is easier to work remotely, so that has moved on hugely. In fact, technology has improved so much that now everyone is constantly connected via their iPhones. The pendulum has swung all the way to the other side!

Maria and Nicolas

My children grew up very self-sufficient, and they knew a lot about my work. They grew up as part of the Deloitte cocoon – they always knew what was going on and felt as though they were part of Deloitte because at home I would talk about my work (obviously nothing confidential), and they would meet my clients at company picnics or dinners. Maria and Nicolas knew about my career, my promotions, my partnership, my colleagues' names. We went to company events when the kids were invited. They loved going to football games, especially when their team Arsenal played. At that time, Deloitte only had a company box at Tottenham, Arsenal's arch-rival, so I used to take them to the match whenever Arsenal played Tottenham, even though the games were typically rough! When Deloitte took over Andersen, Andersen had a company box at the Arsenal stadium, so from that time onwards, I only requested tickets to Arsenal. Both Maria and Nicolas continue to be passionate supporters of Arsenal; they both have season tickets, so they don't miss any matches!

After Maria started at a Church of England primary school, Nicolas also joined; it was easier to get into the school if you had a sibling already there. They both did very well, and Maria was set to move to the next stage, the eleven-plus exams, so she could move up to the high school. She applied to some private schools and two local state schools with a good reputation. She managed to get offers from all of them apart from one private school, which was an excellent achievement. In the end, she decided to go to Haberdashers' Aske's (Habs) School for Girls in Elstree. She loved the school, the gardens, and the teachers and pupils she met.

With Nicolas, things were more complicated. Although he was happy and doing well at St Paul's, we were told that we could do even better if he moved to a local private school called Keble Prep. After a lot of deliberation, thinking that we were doing the right thing for Nicolas, we moved him to Keble at age eight. The new school had a programme that meant the boys were there until they were thirteen, so they sat their exams outside the eleven-plus intakes. At the time, we didn't think much of it, but later, once Nicolas was at Keble, we realised that the school choices at thirteen were less than at eleven, so with his agreement, we decided to prepare him for the eleven-plus intake by having extra lessons so that he would sit the exams at eleven. He really liked Haberdashers' Aske's Boys' School, having been there many times to visit Maria at the girls' school, so he only sat the Habs entrance exam. He was successful with good exam results and Nicolas finally moved from Keble to Habs at age eleven. The headmaster at Keble wasn't very happy with this move, and even though Nicolas had performed so well at the entrance exam at Habs without the assistance of his school, they were not at all nice or indeed professional about it. Nicolas wasn't happy there, so he was delighted to leave Keble and he never looked back!

We knew that some of the parents in our circle were very involved in their children's schoolwork, but our children were confident in doing their work on their own. Those were the days before the Internet era, but the children would go to the library to get additional information about various subjects. Outside regular English school, Maria and Nicolas had piano and swimming lessons, and attended Greek school. I helped them with their Greek, and under my tutelage, they became very good at both reading and writing in Greek. Maria and Nicolas were always ahead of the rest of their year group and were moved up one class. They used to attend Greek school on Saturdays for three hours from two to five, and then the year before they sat their Greek GCSEs, they also had to attend on Wednesdays between 6 and 8pm. Because I could not leave work that early, Philip would come from work early to take them to school or sometimes if he could not make it, another friend would take them, and Philip would collect all the children and drop them off to their respective homes. A lot of our friends' children were doing speech and drama, tap dancing and ballet – I said, 'Forget all that, we don't have time. You do piano, swimming and Greek!' To me, the rest was just peripheral; unless you have real talent and might grow up to be a ballerina or a tennis player, there is no point. Their grandparents took them to swimming classes during the week and Philip took them to piano lessons on Friday evenings. They only stopped piano lessons just before their A-levels started and they had to dedicate more time to their studying. Maria and Nicolas stayed at Habs to take their A-levels. During these years, apart from working and studying hard, Maria was on the lacrosse and netball teams; she continues to play netball at Mishcon de Reya, where she currently works, and has been the captain of the Mishcon team for many years. Nicolas also had a wonderful time at Habs and was very athletic throughout. He was chosen to be on the A team for rugby and through school, he toured South Africa and several European cities, which provided an invaluable experience to him.

When they were growing up, we had our annual four-week holidays in August in Cyprus and sometimes we would send Maria and Nicolas ahead of us, so they would have two weeks or so before we arrived. I loved seeing them relive the experiences I had there as a child. It was just like watching myself at that age – running around the village, doing the kinds of things that kids do in the summer! One year, Maria went to a camp outside Limassol with the Greek school in London as part of the Cypriot Government's Education Ministry, and there she met Greek Cypriot girls and boys from all over the world. When they were older, we took them to Australia, South Africa and the US. We visited New Orleans and Houston to show them the house where we lived and the hospital where they were born. By that time, we were financially comfortable and able to do these long-distance trips as a family; we had moved to our current house and were very happy there.

Neither Maria nor Nicolas was interested in following my profession, and they did not wish to study medicine either. Maria loved Classics and decided to follow a career in law, but she wanted to study Classics first – and we agreed because having a Classics degree would be very useful for law. When Maria was doing her A-level in Classics she had the opportunity to go on a Classics trip to Greece and so I encouraged her to say yes. In the summer of 2000, we went to Athens where the tour started. Maria and I, Maria's close friend Caroline who was also studying Classics for her A-level, and a reluctant Nicolas all went along. We spent a week going all over the main Classical sights in Greece from Athens to Delphi and Olympia. At the end of the week, Caroline returned to London while the kids and I went to the island of Skiathos for a five-day holiday to relax. We had a great time, although our main memory from that trip was that our hotel was at the top of a hill and to come all the way to the beach we had to climb down and climb back up at the end of the day, which was unfortunately over two hundred steps! In addition, as soon as we sat down for breakfast or dinner, a thousand bees surrounded us, very determined to get into our food. Invariably both Maria and Nicolas would start screaming and refuse to sit down at the same table. This was a daily recurrence which lost its funny aspect after the first couple of days! Meanwhile, Philip had to stay home because the renovations we were making to the kitchen were at a critical stage and the downstairs windows were open, so he couldn't leave the builders without supervision. We still refer to that fateful holiday when we were attacked by bees!

The years flew by and before we knew it, they were both at university in Birmingham. Neither of them wanted to study in London. Nicolas liked the idea of studying Economics at the LSE, as I had, but eventually they both went to Birmingham because they liked the campus lifestyle! Nicolas was always less anxious than his sister with regards to studying. We were worried that he mightn't do well at his A-levels because he loved all types of sports, particularly football, so we were concerned that he wasn't studying hard enough to achieve the grades needed for university. In the end, he got the same grades as Maria, two As and one B, which was what Birmingham asked for, so all was well. After his Economics degree, he didn't want to do a master's degree or an MBA but preferred to seek employment after a year out. He finished his degree with a 2:1 so he was set to go travelling and then apply for jobs on his return, contrary to our advice to apply for a job and get something agreed before travelling.

Nicolas is very charming, witty and empathetic, and has great interpersonal skills. He took a job at HSBC in their private banking business and stayed there for five years, where he learned a lot and was successful in that role. When a couple of his close colleagues (his boss and another peer) left, he decided it was time to move to another financial institution, so he moved to Deutsche Bank in their wealth management business, continuing to specialise in providing investment advisory services to high-net-worth individuals (HNWIs). After six years at Deutsche Bank, he left in December 2017 for a smaller firm, Bellecapital. He is very happy at this smaller firm, which is more entrepreneurial, more nimble and more able to offer a wider range of services to their clients than a larger bank with more bureaucracy and regulatory restrictions. Maria also finished her degree with a 2:1, after which she undertook a conversion to law course before joining Mishcon de Reya, a very successful City-based law firm. She opted to specialise in immigration and made partner at the young age of thirty-five, in April 2016. For Maria to make partner so young is a very big deal. I made partner at thirty-nine, because I had a five-year period of employment in Houston which didn't count towards my new career, and I had to start from scratch.

Maria and Nicolas had everything they wanted, but within reason: we didn't spoil them; everything was measured. The early years were tough when we had the mortgage and school fees to pay, but with every passing year as a Deloitte partner, things got better; still, we never wanted them to take what they had for granted. The kids turned out very well. They had the love of their grandparents, and they had their dad around all the time. Because of their grandparents, they had that unconditional love, the spoiling that comes with the grandparent-grandchild relationship. As they grew older, they became very proud of their parents. I think Philip has a unique success story on his side, becoming a professor in 2003 at the age of fifty-one and being awarded the Excellence in Epilepsy Lifetime Achievement Award in 2017 for his contribution to epilepsy care and research. I was made a partner in 1995 under forty, which was my big goal, and Maria is now a partner in her early thirties.

When I went travelling, Maria and I were always a pair. Nicolas sometimes had work commitments or other things that meant he couldn't come, but Maria and I were more adventurous. We get on very well, and everywhere I went, we went together, so it was natural that she would come with me to Nepal and Kilimanjaro. I love being with Maria; it's such great fun – but one thing about her is that, when we are travelling, she always wants to get up as late as possible! She always argued that I worried too much. But Nicolas had a close call when he was leaving Santiago in Chile to go to the airport to catch a flight for Asia and join his friends for their year out. The wake-up call from the hotel's reception was never made; this was before iPhones! Fortunately, he just about made the flight!

We also had a problem with Maria once when we were coming back from the Galapagos Islands. The timing was quite tricky because Maria had to get back to the UK for her partnership interview on Tuesday and we were due to return on Monday evening. At the time of the booking, we had not known that she would be having her partnership interview on that day, and of course, once she knew, she tried to push it back, but they told her that was the deadline, and it could not be moved. As we were coming back from the Galapagos Islands, there was a big thunderstorm and by the time we took off to connect with our airline Iberia via Madrid, and from Madrid to London, we missed the Madrid connection. Iberia was terrible, so unhelpful that I had to write a letter to British Airways afterwards asking how they could be partners with such a useless airline! Eventually, we managed to get Maria the last seat on another flight, so she returned to London before me, and I followed on with all the luggage the following day. She went straight from the airport to the office for her interview in what she was wearing, but it all worked out in the end. Maria became a partner, which was what we all wanted, but getting her back to the UK was an experience I don't think either of us ever want to go through again!

July 2005 (7/7)

Every year at the end of June, we had a Client Expatriate Tax event called the Global Employer Services Tax Client Conference. We had one of these conferences annually in North America, one in EMEA and later one in Asia, but I was primarily responsible for the European conference. I was on the European Advisory Board (EAB). The EAB was comprised by various Deloitte Global Employer Services (GES) leaders across EMEA, plus several of our key GES clients who represented the largest and most prestigious clients for our practice. It was customary for spouses to also attend these meetings. We arrived on Friday afternoon at a nice hotel in a European city, had dinner on Friday night and worked all day Saturday with a lavish dinner on Saturday night. Everyone left on Sunday, which was a relaxing day. We always met in early November of the previous year to start planning the conference agenda, and then the actual conference took place in the third week in June, which was the most convenient time for our clients to attend because of their own timetables.

We chose a different location each year from all the beautiful cities in Europe – Berlin, Düsseldorf, Vienna, Lisbon, Paris, Madrid, Barcelona and London (although not in London that often, since most of the clients attending were based there and they preferred other locations. Furthermore, the cost of holding a conference in London was much higher compared to other destinations). One year, I even convinced them to have it in Athens, and I kept my promise and danced the traditional Greek dances!

In 2005, the conference was in Paris. I was the dean of the conference, one of the two partners who handled the introduction, the announcements for administration and the logistics of the conference. There were usually two partners, a male and a female, who shared that role. For me, the conference always felt like showtime; I would wear my lovely new clothes, and all my clients and colleagues said that they were looking forward to seeing what I was wearing.

That year, Philip and Maria joined me in Paris. Because Philip came to the advisory board meetings, he knew all the clients and my Deloitte colleagues, and he felt very familiar and at home with them. We had a beautiful suite in the hotel in Paris, by the Opera, and we had a fantastic time. I went earlier, because we had an internal global partners' meeting before the clients arrived, where we discussed various issues relating to global tax policies, technical updates and new global changes, so I was there for most of the week. The client conference started on Wednesday lunchtime and finished on Friday lunchtime. Some clients left on Friday while others stayed for the weekend. When my clients stayed for the weekend, we organised tours and dinners on Friday and Saturday. We had a wonderful time, but when we came back to London, I was very tired, because these conferences were quite exhausting events. We got back on Sunday, and I had so much going on that week. Monday and Tuesday were very busy, and on Wednesday night, Philip and I took one of my HSBC clients to the opera to see *Don Giovanni*. During dinner we discussed the awarding of the 2012 Olympics to London, and I recall how Philip was very excited, since he planned to retire beforehand and attend as many events as possible!

By the time we got to Wednesday, I was so exhausted I said to Philip, 'I'm going to stay home on Thursday and work from home.' I never did that, because I was always so busy and so committed, I never got a chance to work from home, but on that day, I was planning to go for a run, go to my Pilates class and have a quiet day working. I even rearranged my Pilates class in Muswell Hill; the instructor, Karen, was surprised to hear that I was available during the day.

On Thursdays, Philip normally worked at the Chalfont Centre for Epilepsy in Chalfont St Peter's in Buckinghamshire, where he spent two days a week. The rest of the week he worked at the National Hospital for Neurology and Neurosurgery in Central London, at Queen Square. However, that day he had an appointment at 9am with the Dean at the Institute of Neurology (part of University College London, where Philip still has his professorial chair). Because I was staying at home that day, our routine was different from the usual. Normally, I got up at quarter past six, the car picked me up at seven and then Philip got up at seven after I left. That day, he stayed longer in bed because his appointment was at 9am, and he was also tired. He said, 'I'll take the later train.' I said, 'Let me know how the meeting goes,' because I knew it was important.

At around ten-thirty, I called his office at the hospital to see how his meeting went, and they said, 'Oh, Ellie, he hasn't arrived yet.' In fact, the Dean's office had been calling to find out where he was because Philip was normally so punctual. I knew this was strange because although he had left home later than usual, he had left plenty of time to be there by nine o'clock. His colleague said to me that they had been told something happened in the Underground, a power failure. I said, 'Oh, maybe that's why he is late. I will put the TV on to listen to the latest news.'

I put the television on, and they were indeed talking about a power surge in the Underground. I thought, 'This must be the reason.' Even now, you cannot use mobiles in the Underground, although there is some Wi-Fi, and back then, mobiles did not work at all. I kept the news on, and it was announced that they now believed that there was something more than a power surge. They were saying that there was an incident northbound on the Piccadilly line, going from Central London to North London. I said, 'Oh my God, I'm so glad Philip is not caught up in that.' I thought he must have been affected by it and that's why he had not been in touch, but I knew he was going in the opposite direction, from our home in North London into Central London. Then the shock came; they corrected the reports and said that the incident happened while the train was going into Central London from North London. Tony Blair, the Prime Minister, was hosting a G7 conference that day and he announced that there was a terrorist attack on the London Underground system and that there were many casualties.

Well, that changed the situation completely. I now realised that he was definitely caught up in whatever happened on the Piccadilly Line, but I was hopeful that with all the chaos that must have transpired, he couldn't call, and he was stuck underground. The news service wasn't clear, so we didn't really know exactly what was happening. Then Maria called and said, 'Mum, where are you?' They all thought I was at work because that is where I would ordinarily be. I said, 'Actually, I'm at home today.'

Maria was just finishing her year out after university and had recently returned from America, where she had a six-month legal internship in New York. Before she had gone to New York, we bought her a flat in Maida Vale, which was where she was living. After she had heard the newscast, she called me to find out whether we were all OK. I had to tell her that I hadn't heard from Dad and explained what had happened, but I was still very positive. I told her, 'Maria, just stay there for now and see what's going on in case you need to go somewhere central to check where Dad is.'

Then Nicolas called from Vietnam. He was also on his year out after university; he and his friends were planning to go to Cambodia after Vietnam and then come home, so by that week in July they only had two weeks before the end of their holiday. He said, 'Mum, are you OK?'

I said, 'Yes, but we haven't heard from Dad for a while.'

He was very upset. I said, 'Well, at the moment, we don't really know what's going on.'

Nicolas said, 'I'm coming home, I'm not going to stay any longer.'

I said, 'Don't rush. Call me later, in a few hours. I may have some more news.'

By that time, all of my family and friends kept calling me from London, Margate and Cyprus. My niece Eleni was in Athens when this happened, and she called me. I said, 'I'm OK, but we haven't heard from Philip yet,' so of course that went viral straight away. Everyone was calling me, and my cousin Tony, who lived in Central London, the son of my aunt Georgina, who lived in Margate, called, and said to me, 'What can I do?'

I said, 'Listen. For the time being, nothing. But I will call you if I need anything from you.'

In the meantime, the TV announcements were unhelpful. They provided an emergency telephone number and said, 'If you are looking for a loved one, call this emergency number,' but it was constantly busy, and nobody picked up the phone.

By that time, it was hours later. Maria kept calling and I said, 'Maria, come home,' because I wanted her there with me, so Maria and a number of my close friends also came to the house. We then heard that the best way to find out information was to call all the hospitals and ask if they had any unidentified victims, so we took turns calling the emergency number as well as calling all the hospitals. My friends at HSBC – John Bond, the chairman, and Mike Geoghegan, the CEO – called me when they realised Philip was missing. They informed the police commissioner, and we had to give them Philip's description. I was trying to remember what he was wearing because I was asleep when he left that morning, but eventually I managed to figure out what he must have been wearing. The High Commissioner of Cyprus based in London called me as well because Philip was the only Cypriot not accounted for, and he reassured me that they were doing all they could to try and find out where he was.

We kept calling the hospitals to see whether they had anybody of his description. They said, 'No.' We thought he would be in University College London Hospital (UCLH) because it was located near Russell Square. Later, we found out that because UCLH was full, they were taking patients to the Royal London Hospital in Whitechapel. When we called UCLH for the hundredth time, they told us that they heard that there were a few unidentified victims at the Royal London Hospital.

Immediately, I called my cousin Tony and said, 'Tony, please go to the Royal London Hospital, because that is the only hospital where they tell us that there are victims still not identified.'

He said, 'OK, I am on my way. I'll call you as soon as I find anything.'

Nicolas called again. This time I said, 'Nicolas, Dad is still missing. Come home.'

By that time, it was 8pm, and the incident had happened at eight-fifty in the morning. It had taken all day. At that time, I thought he must have been dead unless he was at a hospital, and they had not identified him. A few of my very good friends came over and took turns answering the phone. I didn't want to pick up the phone all the time, because there was so much drama. My father, sisters and brothers in Cyprus were all very upset, and we had TV channels calling from Athens and Cyprus. It always happens when there is a big tragedy: people always try to get the real stories, get the victim's family talking about what they are going through. We had that for the next few days after the incident, but that first day we were waiting, trying to get the hospitals to call us back in case they had new information about any new patients coming in.

Tony called around 8:30pm. He said, 'We have found him. He is alive, he is in intensive care. He is swollen all over, I mean, it took me some time to recognise him, but he is alive. He is out of danger, so come over.'

My cousin Stav and her husband Bambos Georgiou drove me to the hospital. On the way there, Tony called me back and he said, 'Before you get here, I want to tell you that Philip has lost one of his legs below the knee. They are looking after him. They don't know yet whether they have to amputate any more. It depends on how he develops.'

I said, 'That's fine.' Honestly, I didn't really think about it; I was convinced he was dead, and to be told that he was still alive was such a relief!

We arrived at the intensive care unit of Royal London Hospital, and I was scared about what I would see. When I saw him, I thought, 'Oh my God.' Each of his fingers was the size of a person's arm, he was that swollen. There was also something else which obviously I had never thought about before – what they called human projectile injuries. Essentially, when a body explodes, parts of that body become embedded in others. He had a tracheotomy and could not breathe, speak at all or open his eyes – he was in a coma. The next day, Nicolas arrived from the Far East, so skinny and dark from travelling, and the three of us, Maria, Nicolas and I, took it in turn to sit with Philip so he always had someone with him.

Unfortunately, they had to keep cutting his injured left leg, because it was getting gangrenous, and eventually they had to cut it above the knee. Our biggest fear was whether he would also lose his right leg. It was very damaged, but the reconstructive surgeon,

Miss Hasu Patel, tried very hard to save it, and she succeeded! Later, he had nightmares and delusions, a side effect of the drugs. He was convinced one of the nurses was trying to kill him, and he was so adamant that the police started an investigation into it, but it was all in his mind. He would write on a blackboard, like a child, to communicate with us, because he could hear but he could not speak because he had a tracheotomy. After twelve days, he was moved from intensive care and taken to a special rehabilitation ward and isolated in a room by himself because he was still very weak and vulnerable to infections. Four days later the tracheal tube was removed, and he slowly began to speak again. On the first day he drank some water and ate a yoghurt; it was a big step in his recovery, and we were all so pleased.

He had a lot of visitors, a lot of friends and colleagues from his work, and our friends and family in the UK. In addition, my sister Miroula, my niece Eleni, her brother Xenakis and my friend Maro came from Cyprus – a lot of people came from all over to support us and be with us. The nurses would say, 'Professor Patsalos, you are the most popular patient we have ever had.' During those days afterwards, I was getting calls from TV channels and newspapers to talk about what happened and how we were coping. I was very brave, but at night, when I was in bed on my own, I was always crying. Philip was discharged home nine weeks and two days after the incident.

The 7/7 bombings involved four individuals with homemade explosives blowing themselves up in Underground carriages at King's Cross/Russell Square, Aldgate and Edgware Road, and a bus in Tavistock Square. Fifty-two people were killed, and many hundreds of people injured. Philip was in a King's Cross/Russell Square carriage where half (twenty-six) of the people had been killed. Philip was only two or three feet from the bomber, and what saved him that day we will never know.

The 7/7 Aftermath

Deloitte provided me with a chauffeur to take me to the hospital and bring me back home, and the chauffeur was available twenty-four seven. After that, I had a chauffeur until I retired. I never went on the Underground again until after that.

Although Philip was still in hospital, I knew I could not stay at home all the time; I would go crazy if I did. I went into work in the morning until about two o'clock, and then the car would take me from work to the hospital. Maria and Nicolas went in the morning because they were not working at the time, and the following day we would do exactly the same routine. On the weekends, I went in the mornings and the kids would come later. We took it in turns. The nurses told us that in all the years they were working at the Royal London, they had never seen a patient have so many visitors every single day, and that made Philip smile!

We got to know some of the other patients who had been injured in the incident, including a young girl in the room next to Philip who had just got engaged to her boyfriend and had lost both of her legs above the knee. Philip left the hospital in late September, and he had been taken there on 7th July, so he was there for close to three months. When he was in the hospital, he was under a lot of supervision and receiving help. He was undergoing physiotherapy and was also being taught how to get in and out of a wheelchair, in and out of bed, and up and down the stairs. We were worried about the house when he came home – whether the doors would be wide enough to go through in a wheelchair. The bed needed reinforcements, the bathroom needed adjustments too – there were all these practical things that we had no clue about, because you never do, until this type of event happens to you.

Even though Philip was depressed in the hospital, he did not really have a chance to think about it and dwell on it because there was so much going on and so many people visiting him and speaking to him. Once we were back at home it was like a hotel; everyone coming in and out all the time, always having to have teas and coffees and cookies available for all the visitors, who would bring gifts, food and drinks to us as well. It was like a party, all these people coming and going, but still, when Philip came home, it really hit him, and he was in a very bad mood. He was very upset and angry – so, so much. At the time he hated the wheelchair even though it was the only way he would move around. He had to go up the stairs on his bum – they showed him how to do that, and how to get from there to the wheelchair. We had a wheelchair upstairs and one downstairs and in front of the house there was a plank of wood we were using as a ramp. On top of that, he had to wait for several months to allow the swollen amputated limb to settle and thus get measured up for an artificial leg.

At the Royal Orthopaedic Hospital in Stanmore, Philip was under the care of Professor Rajiv Hanspal, Consultant in Rehabilitation Medicine, in the limb-fitting department. His first prosthetic leg was not very sturdy because the knee was readily collapsible, and Philip would unexpectedly collapse to the ground. This made me very worried, particularly when I was travelling, and Philip was on his own at home. However, once he got the 'C leg' (computer leg) made in Germany, which had an electronically controlled knee mechanism, the risk of falling was eliminated – unless he tripped over, just like 'normal' people.

Once Philip started walking, he became more confident, but Philip has never been a very optimistic person. He is naturally very measured. His glass is always half-empty, whereas mine is overflowing! But he needed somebody like me to keep pushing him. He would get annoyed at me when I was encouraging him – 'Walk a bit more, do this, you can do more than that!' – but he knew, deep down, that I was doing the right thing for him. We managed. Looking back, I don't know how we did it, but at that time we were just focused on getting through it a day at a time. As usual, the way I dealt with it was through work, just like I did with my illness. I had to keep busy, continue to think about other things, because if you stay home and do nothing it gets worse. That was why it was worse for Philip in the early days, because he had nowhere to go.

I returned to work in October. Earlier, I had been invited to speak at the partners' conference in late September, a few days before Philip was discharged from the hospital. I said yes, and everybody was quite emotional when I showed up. While I had seen quite a few of my colleagues, I had not seen everybody since the incident. It was a huge room full of people, and it was quite an emotional day. I felt very good about that, and how well it had gone. The next time I left the UK to travel, like I had before, was in October. We had the Americas conference in San Francisco, a version of the one we had in Paris before all of this happened. I said to Philip, 'I want to go,' and he said to me, 'Go.' My sister Miroula came from Cyprus, and so she was looking after him and Nicolas, and cooking for them. By that time Maria was working, she had just started at Mishcon in August, so they managed between my sister and Nicolas. I was only gone from Monday to Friday, but it was so good for me to be away for the first time, not worrying constantly.

That December, Philip's boss had a party at his home and we were invited. It was the first time that Philip had driven a car and had gone out to a social gathering since the incident. We went to the party, and Philip's colleagues were all very happy to see him. It was very emotional for Philip to see so many of his colleagues and to be able to walk.

Earlier in 2004, we had bought a house in Cyprus on the beach which was being built and was expected to be completed in the summer of 2005. We were planning to have a big beach party; we had chosen the date, 9th August, and Eleni was organising the invitations. We planned the catering, the music and everything, but of course it all had to be cancelled after the 7th July disaster. We went to Cyprus for Christmas that year instead. My father was still alive at the time, and by then Philip had started walking on his first artificial leg. That Christmas he was wobbling on the new leg and my father was holding on to his own walking frame. They staggered towards each other and embraced, both crying. It was a very emotional reunion. It was also the first time we moved into our new house in Cyprus. That was the only time in my career as a partner that I took four weeks off, and it was wonderful to have some quiet time. We had a magical time with Maria, Nicolas and all our family and friends. We were all thankful above everything that Philip had survived!

Philip has never agreed to speak to anyone about his experience on that awful day and the subsequent huge changes to his life. I was contacted by *Panorama, National Geographic*, all the prestigious papers and channels, from Cyprus, Greece and here in the UK. On one occasion I agreed to speak to a Greek channel; I was not rude, but I did not encourage them either, just answered their questions. Philip was approached to tell his story at the six-month anniversary, and then at the one-year anniversary and subsequent anniversaries, and we often had journalists knock on our doorstep asking for an interview with Philip. Philip said no to it all. He was very adamant. He decided that he would maintain his privacy and get on with his life without the intrusion of the media.

Philip returned to work in the following year, on 11th June 2006, months after 7/7, and his interaction with his colleagues and patients proved to be therapeutic. At that time, technology was getting better, so he could do a lot more work from home, and colleagues were constantly visiting and keeping him informed of work matters and also bringing him work. At first, he went to work a couple of days a week, then three days and gradually he went full time.

I started to travel again, and Nicolas started a new job in January 2006, in HSBC's private banking area. Shortly after that, we helped him buy his first flat and he moved to Notting Hill. Philip did not want him to move out, because he was very comfortable having him around and he was good company. I said to Philip, 'You have to let him go, like Maria. It's not right for him to stay here forever.' Maria had other issues at the time that made her want to leave, which we were not fully aware of then, but it was different for Nicolas, being a boy and the younger child. Boys tend to prefer the amenities of home and the ease of being taken care of by their mums! He left more reluctantly than Maria, but Philip was still not happy and told me, 'You should not have encouraged him to go.' I said, 'He should not just stay here because you enjoy having a nice chat with him in the evenings! Nicolas has to get on with his own life.'

At the one-year anniversary of the 7/7 bombings, Prince Charles held an event at his summer house outside London, in Sandringham. It was attended by people who were directly affected by the incident and those that contributed to their survival and wellbeing. By this time the victims that had lost legs were starting to walk with the use of their prosthetic limbs, and they were like kids, wobbly – Philip was walking and spotted the girl that he knew from his stay at the Royal London Hospital, and the two of them started to walk towards each other. They almost fell on top of each other and we had to hold them up! It was funny and sad at the same time.

Every year at the anniversary of the incident on 7th July we have been having a celebration get-together. It has been attended by various survivors along with their spouses and various doctors, police liaison officers, ambulance personnel, physiotherapists, prosthetists, and other members of the public that aided us and helped us survive the trauma. Some of the people who were injured do not live in London, but they happened to be caught in one of the three trains and one bus explosion. One lady who lost her arm lives outside London and was in London for the day on business, and another survivor came to London for the day for a conference, and he was caught up in the Aldgate explosion. There were so many other people involved whom we grew close to during that time. Every family had two liaison officers, and police officers to make sure everything was OK and support us in whatever we needed, as well as Miss Hasu Patel, the reconstructive surgeon, who undertook many surgeries on the survivors admitted to the Royal London Hospital. She had such a sweet smile throughout, encouraging everyone to be positive. She published a great deal of research in the following years because doctors in the UK had not seen injuries like that since the tragic IRA bombings in the 1970s, so she learned so much from doing these operations. She always had an encouraging smile and Philip said while he was in the hospital, he would see these beautiful eyes looking down at him, and that was Miss Patel. She was so amazing with all the patients.

Every year Philip also invites Professor Rajiv Hanspal, who was the Consultant in Rehabilitation Medicine at the Royal Orthopaedic Hospital in Stanmore where Philip's rehabilitation work took place and who worked with him and helped with the prosthetics. Every other year, Maria and Nicolas come with us, and Philip always gives a speech and highlights how we had all made progress in our lives – there have been marriages and newly born children. They are in a good place.

Still, no matter what, Philip's quality of life has been severely compromised and he constantly has challenges in his everyday life. He never really got to enjoy our house on the beach in Cyprus; to freely walk along the beach and swim in the sea unaided. Nevertheless, he is alive and that is paramount. I was almost glad that his mother Maria died in November 2004 in her sleep and was not alive to see what happened to her beloved son.

Losing Eleni

Not long after that, we lost Eleni, my beautiful niece whom I used to look after as a child when we went to stay in the mountains. She fought the cancer for a long time, but I remember the day we realised this was it. It had spread to her liver, so we went to see a specialist for a second opinion; before she started the treatment recommended by her doctor (using a similar technology to microwave heat to kill part of the cancer) she wanted to see if it was possible to have part of her liver removed, since the liver could regenerate itself.

That day, Eleni, her husband Costantinos and I went to see the specialist with all the X-rays already done, and all the information provided by her doctor in Cyprus. Initially, the specialist was very bullish, but when he saw her X-rays and scans, he said, 'I can't do anything for you. It's not just in the liver, but all over. I am so sorry, but the best way forward is to proceed with the treatment already recommended to you.' We were all stunned by his words because it became clear that it was now only a matter of time. Now it was no longer a question of whether she was going to fight the cancer, but how long she had left. Once we left the hospital, we hugged her and started crying.

After that, we kept going back to St Thomas's Hospital, where I had my original operation. The doctor – a Greek doctor, as it happened – performed a procedure where they microwaved part of the liver, effectively killing the cancer. However, because the liver is so close to other key organs, he could not microwave all of it in case her other organs were affected. Although the procedure was initially successful, after a few months the cancer would reappear and the whole process would start again. Eleni continued with this procedure, as well as chemotherapy, for several years.

In 2006, she went on a trip with me – attending an annual client tax conference in Shanghai, also visiting Hong Kong and Singapore, because she had never been to Asia before and wanted to visit Asia so badly! We had a fantastic time together, she met and charmed my Deloitte colleagues and clients, but I could tell she was getting very tired; her skin was very pale and her hair very thin. The usual energetic Eleni wasn't there. We came back to London on 30th April, and then on 1st May she flew back to Cyprus to attend her eldest niece Thekla's christening. On 21st May, Greece was hosting the Eurovision Song Contest in Athens and because we happened to be in Cyprus and in Eleni's house when the Greek song 'My Number One', sung by Helena Paparizou, won, we said that the following year, we would all go to Athens for Eurovision, so I got tickets for myself, Maria and Nicolas. Eleni and our other friends couldn't make it, so the day of the final contest I called Eleni on her mobile but there was no response. I thought that was odd, so I called her over and over, but it went to voicemail. After trying to contact her unsuccessfully all morning, I called my sister Youla, who started crying as soon as I said hello. She told me that Eleni was in a very serious condition in hospital, and the doctor was not hopeful. I talked to Costantinos, who was more hopeful, but I couldn't speak to Eleni. That evening I didn't enjoy Eurovision at all; my mind was on Eleni. I decided that on Sunday, rather than returning to London with the children, I would fly to Cyprus instead to see Eleni and then go back home.

I flew to Cyprus on my birthday, 22nd May, and went straight to the oncological hospital where she was admitted. I stayed with her in the hospital that night and slept on the bed next to her. Her liver wasn't functioning properly, so her stomach was bloated and they kept draining it. She knew very well that once they couldn't drain the liver all the toxic waste would spread and that would be the end. We talked all night, and she knew the end was near. She asked me to look after her two sons, Giorgos and Savvas, and stay close to Costantinos, who would need someone strong next to him. The following day they allowed her to go home so I spent all day with her. Her sister Eleftheria and I took her for a car ride to the sea front; she wanted to see the water. She was so happy when we returned home. On 25th May, I returned to London, and I remember she was in her bed when I waved to her and told her that I would see her the following month for our summer holiday. She responded with a sad smile and told me, 'I hope so, but I don't think so.'

On 28th May it was a bank holiday in London, and I received a call from a close friend of Eleni's and mine, Marianna, who told me that I should get to Cyprus as soon as possible because Eleni would not last more than twenty-four hours. I was very shocked because although I kept very close to my sister and Costantinos, I hadn't been told she was that bad. I guess they were both in denial! I went into the office, sorted out the more important things I had to do, sent emails to my partners and my secretary, and flew to Cyprus with Philip that afternoon. Eleni's brother-in-law George was waiting for us at the airport in Larnaca and we went straight to the hospital in Nicosia. Eleni was asking about Philip and me and whether we were there; she was waiting for us before she was ready to go.

We entered the room where she was lying, and she was so white and serene. She looked at me and she smiled, and then saw Philip and smiled again. I kissed her and said goodbye. Once she saw us, she closed her eyes, still smiling, and went into a coma.

She died a few hours later, still looking so calm and happy, as if she was sleeping and having a lovely dream.

It was 29th May when she died, twenty-eight days after we returned from our trip in the Far East. When we were travelling together, her cancer was at the very last stage and she knew, I think, that she didn't have much time left. Her funeral was very difficult for all of us. Maria and Nicolas came for a couple of days to be there because they both loved her so much. She was such an amazing person and made everyone feel so special. Maria and Nicolas loved Eleni; she was just an amazing force of nature. Though she was older than them, she would always make them laugh and she would be very modern, loving and giving. Of course, we have a lot of wonderful people in the family, but Eleni was a special jewel, and I know if you asked Maria and Nicolas, they would say the same thing.

Recognition

Life went on, and so did work. One of my greatest achievements came when I was made vice-chairman. John Connolly, our CEO, decided which senior partners should be considered for the vice-chairman position. To be considered, you had to be a successful senior partner, and being successful in that context meant having all the ingredients of excellent client services, successful financially and recognised as the best in your area of expertise internally and in the marketplace externally. When I was made vice-chairman, I was the second woman in that role; Margaret Ewing was already a vice-chair. She was a very experienced FS senior audit partner who went into industry as a CFO and then returned to Deloitte. She was an amazing woman and a close friend of mine. As mentioned earlier, she was part of the Women in Leadership team set up by the CEO a few years earlier.

Another example of my recognition by the firm was that during our annual partners' conference in June 2008, we celebrated a huge financial landmark. Our firm had had an exceptional year and we managed to hit the £1 billion revenue mark, so we were celebrating! We had a famous pianist perform in late morning, and after the piano performance, the doors to the huge room opened and waiters rushed in with big trays full of champagne. To top this off, after the lunch break, John Connolly announced that year's two top outstanding partners. A year earlier, he had started giving an award to the most successful partners (two each year) according to him. It was his choice and decision as to who had the best year in their careers for the benefit of our firm and our clients. He was very secretive, to the extent that only his trusted PA knew the names engraved on the prizes presented! John was always a great supporter of mine. He knew all my clients who always praised me and told him that, 'Ellie is great, you're so lucky to have a partner like her.' Of course, he knew all my results and internationally, when he attended the global meetings, all the CEOs of the various countries I was visiting for my clients were mentioning my name. 2008 was the second year that he had presented this award. I remember I was wearing a pink dress, and I had just had my hair done because we had the gala dinner that evening, and I thought, 'I wonder whether I will get this...' and I heard my name! I still have the lovely plaque with my name engraved.

It was a lovely sunny and warm day when I received the award. We were at the Hilton in Park Lane and after that session, during our coffee break, I walked across to Hyde Park and I called Maria, Nicolas and Philip, but no one was picking up. Then I called my friend Maro in Cyprus, who picked up, but she didn't fully understand what an amazing achievement it was! I then called Egly, my university classmate, and had a long discussion. It was the icing on the cake, to be selected out of all the partners in the whole firm! The other partner, Cahal Dowds, a great friend based in Scotland, was the other recipient. That night, after dinner, we celebrated in style!

John Connolly had been old-fashioned in some ways, but he was an iconic CEO, and we had seen extraordinary growth and change under him. When he left, there was a big gap to fill. We all felt it was time for a change and John had served the maximum time he could. He was the one who had been bullish enough to take in Arthur Andersen in 2002. Andersen had originally been talking to KPMG and not Deloitte, but KPMG had second thoughts and did not go ahead with the deal, so John Connolly came in and closed the deal very quickly. He was aggressive, and it was risky, but the firm received legal advice from Freshfields, who gave us the green light, and so we went ahead with it. All the partners had to vote, but we all trusted John on this huge issue and he was right. Unfortunately, I was away on a business trip, so I missed all the excitement, but I voted via proxy, authorising our chairman to vote yes for me. John was a risk-taker, but a very seasoned decision-maker. He would look at all the options and discuss matters with the partners and the board, and then a final decision was taken.

When John was retiring, we had a choice between supporting a younger partner who could be closer to our partners or appointing an older and very experienced partner. When the time came to choose whom to support, I preferred to go for somebody forward-looking from Arthur Andersen, and that somebody was David Sproul. He was the Head of Tax, so I knew him quite well. I told him, 'I only want to do what is best for the firm. I think you will be the better person for the next ten years.' It was good for him that he had a senior partner at Deloitte supporting him. He had all the Andersen partners, but he wanted someone senior from Deloitte to assist him in his candidacy. I was a member of the board, and I had a lot of influence in tax and the other service lines since I dealt with so many partners and clients. When he was finally elected, we stayed close and he was very supportive; he trusted me.

For us, the financial crisis had a delayed effect. The crisis happened in 2007–2008, and in 2008, we had our best year ever – but we felt the crunch two to three years later, when companies started cutting back. For example, during that period, we would charge some clients less than the full rates to help them. It was a tough time for our clients, but some of them brought it on themselves, the investment banking businesses in particular. The people that created all those artificial loan notes that no one understood were not behaving properly and took on too much risk without keeping their boards and leadership abreast of the potential catastrophic consequences. They did not understand what was happening, that was the problem.

I remember it was a Friday, and I was meeting with my client from Deutsche Bank; he was the Head of Investment Banking. It was summertime, and I was ready to go on holiday that weekend. He said, 'This is not good, but I hope the markets will have calmed down by the time we are all back from the summer holidays'. But of course it was the beginning of a deep recession, and they suffered like everyone in the City.

However, even under those circumstances, financial institutions had to put different policies in place such as cost-cutting and they needed us to help implement their cost-cutting strategies. Whichever way things were going, big firms like Deloitte were always doing well. There was also a need for reorganisations and risk processes had to be implemented. Maybe we did a little less well because some of the companies we worked with were struggling or the smaller clients could no longer afford us, but the big multinational companies still needed firms like Deloitte, whether the news was good or bad. If companies had regulatory problems, they needed help, and that was their number-one priority because if they were non-compliant in that area in the US, they had to spend whatever money was needed to remedy their processes and keep them going. Whether it was cost-cutting by offshoring or finding savings in the services provided, companies needed expertise. They needed assistance with automation and help to upgrade their systems; every way you look at it, in every aspect of their business, they needed outside specialist consulting services.

Also, the Big Four professional firms were very nimble; they reinvented themselves and went into areas that had high demand. Four years before I retired, the focus was on digital analytics, the ability to look at a lot of data and take relevant findings to make a story and get results. That was huge, and I was always amazed at what information they could deduce from this humongous amount of data. Now, the focus is on robotics. Some of the audit and bookkeeping tasks are quite repetitive and can potentially be done by robots. The audit industry has undergone a big transformation because of the financial crisis. The financial regulator was challenging the audit firms as to why they'd missed all the signs and risks inherent in the banks' accounts during their audits, so the accounting profession came under the public spotlight, and because of that, they changed a lot of rules about what auditors can and cannot do for their audit clients. For example, they limited the provision of services other than audit and they introduced rotation of audit firms after seven years. Because of the need to change audit firms, there have been a plethora of audit bids which cost so much for each firm, and with the restriction on being able to provide other services meaning that the audit practice is not profitable now, so the profitable parts of the firm, such as consulting and tax, are not happy and there is talk about separating the audit practice from the rest of the accounting firms. This challenge continues and brings back memories of the Andersen split from Andersen Consulting decades ago, now known as Accenture.

In those years, my day-to-day life was hectic but amazing. When I was in London, I left home at seven o' clock by car and on the way to the office I would contact my colleagues or clients in Asia since they were up by then, or I would be reading materials or reports or catching up on my technical reading! There was never a dull moment. When I went in to work, it was back-to-back meetings with partners, with clients, with the board. I would be looking at bids, reviewing draft presentations for my many responsibilities, agendas for the monthly GFSI/EMEA calls and preparing for client visits in the UK or overseas. In addition, while in London, I was always busy socialising, whether that was breakfast, lunch, dinner or events – I would go to everything from football in the evenings and weekends, rugby at Twickenham, tennis at Wimbledon, to theatre, opera and dinners, and to special events Deloitte organised, such as client and speaking events. It was relentless. Sometimes I realised I had to change my plans because I had to be in such-and-such a country for a meeting or presentation. We had tax conferences, financial services conferences, client conferences; it was just so much. I had at least two trips to Asia per year, New York minimum four times a year, Latin America twice a year, and then on top of that I had to go to specific conferences; I was here, there and everywhere. I travelled much more than I do now, although I still travel a lot. I would do short trips as well, and for example, I would go to Brussels, Paris, Zurich or Amsterdam and back on the same day. It was a crazy time. Because my kids had left home by then, I was always working, and I enjoyed it. I said to myself, 'I can't stop now, because I have so much, and if I don't do it now, no one will do it for me. I have to do it.' I also had to prepare many appraisals, because I had so many people reporting to me since I was involved in so many areas, and with the global partners, not just the UK partners. The pace accelerated gradually. When I was a younger partner, I would go to Asia for two weeks. Now it's a week maximum; a week is a long time. Although the pace accelerated, it was not frightening because every year was busier, and every month was busier, and every day was busier, but somehow, I coped. Still, it was a good kind of busy. Sometimes you have challenges and not everything goes well: you worry that you are going to lose a client, or a member of your team is leaving, but you get through it.

When we renovated one of our buildings, Stonecutter Court, we included a large gym in the basement, which was used a lot by the partners and all our staff. I used a personal trainer, a young man called Nick who really pushed me. I was always fit and ran at least three times per week. While I was working, all I could do was go to the Deloitte gym after work and run at the weekends. When I was travelling, I always took my running gear with me and went to the hotel gym if I had time. In Asia, I always made time because I ate so much, breakfast, lunch and dinner all the time. There was so much entertaining everywhere I went! Overall, I thrived in this hectic lifestyle. Some people were intimidated and couldn't cope, but I thrived. Maria is like me in that way.

Changing Expectations

When the kids were growing up in the eighties, Philip and I still had the mentality that meant we expected Maria to get married to a Greek Cypriot boy and Nicolas to a Greek Cypriot girl. Not even to a Greek – it specifically had to be a Greek Cypriot. We felt that as the children were socialising and interacting with so many young Greek people at Greek school and in our wider circle of friends, then, surely, they would meet somebody they liked. But of course, that doesn't always happen. If you grow up with kids that are very close to you and you interact with them often, you see them as friends, not romantically, and that is exactly what happened with our two. At one stage Nicolas liked one of the girls from Greek school, but it didn't go anywhere. When the kids went to university, our views changed. We thought, if they marry somebody educated, somebody professional and similar to them, it did not matter if they were English or Italian or American. You become more accepting.

Maria spent more time in Cyprus than Nicolas because he had to go to South Africa on his rugby tour and did a few work placements in the summer, and so he missed a few of the trips to Cyprus and his Greek wasn't as good as Maria's. Because she was spending so much more time in Cyprus and meeting people, and she spoke the language well, I was quite certain at the time that Maria would marry a Greek Cypriot boy. I knew she would miss the UK if she left, unless she met the right boy and then of course everything might change, but those were the only circumstances under which I could see her living in Cyprus.

It was the same with Nicolas. We felt that if he met the right girl and was willing to go to Cyprus we would support them, because I knew they would have a good quality of life and they would be financially able to travel wherever they wanted, just like my friends who had grown up in Cyprus and gone to the LSE to do their degrees. I felt like this was something positive to bear in mind, but I knew that in Cyprus they would never have the kind of opportunities that living in the UK presents. There is no way I could compare my life and my career to that of my friends in Cyprus. It's a different life, a different dimension. It could be that the children would be happy or even happier in Cyprus than in the UK, but the breadth of experiences and relationships – it's just not the same.

We always had a rule that we would not meet any of the children's boyfriends or girlfriends unless they were serious about them. They would tell us sometimes if they liked someone, but we were not interested in meeting peripheral girlfriends and boyfriends, and we had the same rule for both Maria and Nicolas. There was no point in seeing people they were not genuinely serious about. For instance, our friends in Birmingham, Androulla and Kostakis, have three boys, and they became close to their sons' girlfriends. Then when they broke up it was very tough on everybody because you get attached, and Philip and I didn't want to go through that.

By the time Maria went to university, we were concerned that she had not had many boyfriends. She had met one boy in Cyprus through her cousins whom she really liked. He came to Oxford for a second degree, so they met a few times. Maria visited him in Oxford, and he came to London a couple of times, and then it was off. We don't know what happened; she never told us. Maria was very silent about that part of her life. We would try to introduce her to boys and sometimes she would go on a date with them, but often she refused because she did not think they were her type.

After university, Maria stayed on for an extra year for her law conversion course, and then she came back to London and did her LPC, the legal requirement that you must complete before you apply for a legal contract. After that, all Maria's friends were taking a year out, but she planned to go to America for an internship with the law firm Willkie Farr and Gallagher. I knew the law firm because they had worked with me on the Bloomberg account. I took Maria to New York, and we chose a beautiful apartment across from where she was working. All her colleagues were very envious – work started at 9:30, and then at 9:27am, Maria would walk across to the office, and she was home in two minutes afterwards! It was the first time she lived in the US as an adult and she absolutely loved it, though she missed out on the year out that some of her friends took, going travelling. After she came back from New York, her apartment in Maida Vale was ready, so she moved from New York to her new flat. She joined some friends in early summer in Asia for ten days or so. Shortly after she came back, Philip was involved in the 7/7 incident, while she was in London waiting to start her contract at Mishcon de Reya. As mentioned earlier, Nicolas was in Vietnam when he heard the news about the explosion and the terrorist attack. He cut his travels short and he returned to London, which was good timing because Maria had to start work and Nicolas could assist me in looking after Philip.

Maria told us that she was gay when she was in her late twenties. I remember it was 30th November, and we had just been to Raphaela's and Sophia's (our goddaughters) birthday party. Every November they had a party in their house and invited all the family and friends. That day, we came back from the celebrations, and we were in the house, and I could see Maria was a bit on edge. She asked Philip to join us and said, 'I want to tell you something.'

I said, 'OK,' and called Nicolas in from the kitchen to sit down with us.

When she told us she was gay, we were shocked, even though deep down Philip and I had suspected so, because we had not seen or heard about any boyfriends in a long time. The last one was that boy from Cyprus, and at one point she told us she was seeing a Russian boy for a while.

We were very upset, crying and still in shock. She said, 'Would you feel better if I told you I had breast cancer?'

And we said, 'Of course not, we love you and we will support you.'

Philip asked Maria as to her various intentions including whether she planned to have a baby, and she said yes, she did, which pleased us both. After Maria and Nicolas left, the shock hit us. Philip was so distraught, he would not even shave to go to work; he was really very upset by it. By the next few days, we had many questions to ask Maria and thus we asked her to come home one evening after work so that we could discuss matters further. Philip was quite angry, while I was on the fence; I was also very upset but not in the same way as Philip. That evening we discussed many matters at length, and by the end of the evening we all understood the reality that we faced.

Shortly afterwards, I talked to my friends Shamim Sarif and Hanan Kattan, a gay couple I had met after Shamim spoke at an event at Deloitte. I arranged a meeting with them, and I was crying when I told them about Maria, but at the same time I was aware that I was talking to a gay couple who had a fantastic twenty-year marriage and two sons. They tried to comfort me, told me it would be all right and that I should accept Maria's decision. There was also a female partner at Deloitte, Kalvinder, who was gay – her brother was gay too – and she told me how her parents

1985, full family photo in Aradippou: Ellie and her six siblings with their mum and dad

1985, Ellie, Philip, Maria, Nicolas and Ellie's mum and dad in Aradippou

2004, Ellie with her niece Eleni and best friend Maro visiting London while Eleni was having cancer treatment

August 2013 at Coworth Park, Ascot at Nicolas and Maria's engagement party

November 2013 in Nepal, trekking with Maria and close friend Marigay McKee

September 2014 at the Anassa Hotel in Paphos, Cyprus, for Nicolas & Maria's wedding

2020, Iris at five months old

August 2020 at Aynhoe Park Hotel in Oxfordshire.
Top: Maria and Nisrine on their wedding day; bottom: family photo.

VII

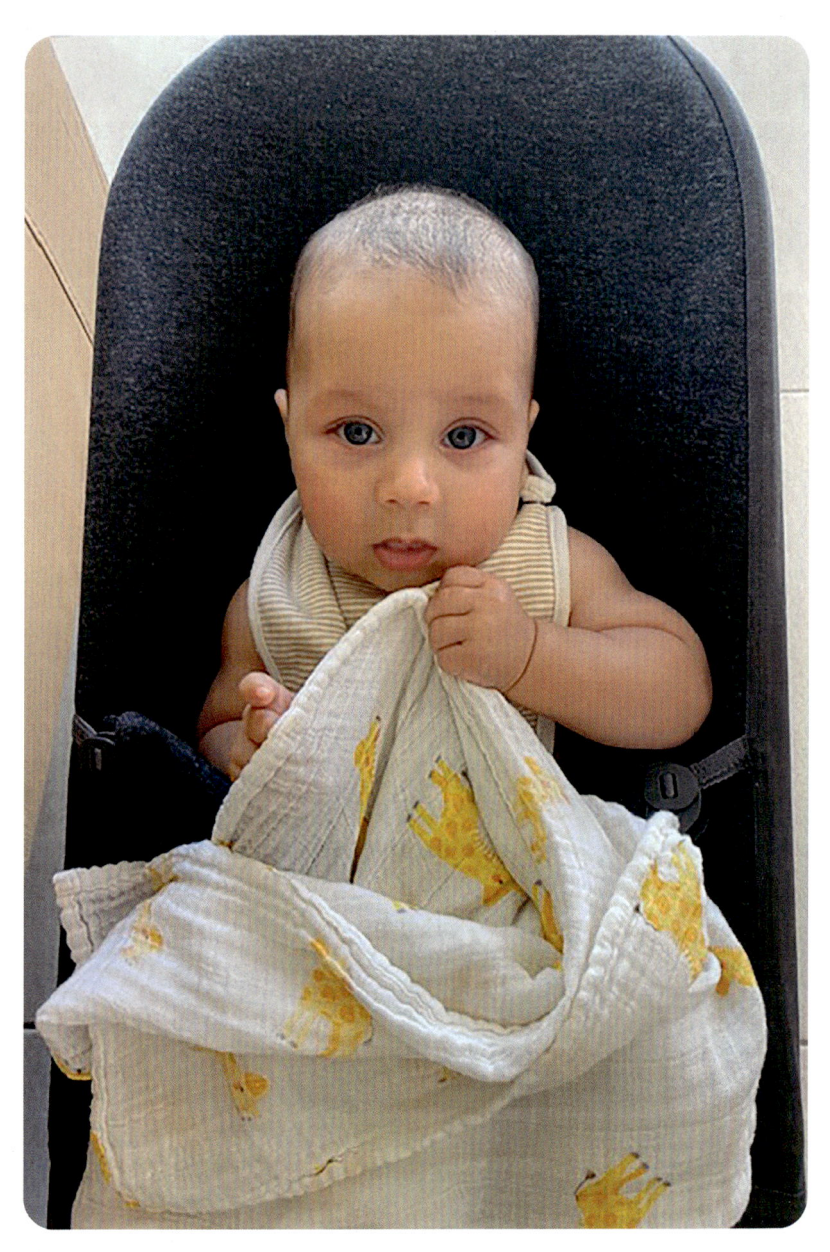

Raphael at three months old

reacted. For us, it took some time. During the early stages, Maria was doing the skydive for the Breakthrough Cancer charity that I'd done the year before, and at that time she was going out with her girlfriend Alex. We went to support Maria when she did the skydive and Alex was there. Philip was polite and had a good conversation with her. That was the first time that he'd seen Alex, so it was quite early in their relationship, and after that she came to our house a few times and had lunch with us, and Philip and I became more accepting. We needed time to get used to it, to absorb it, to get comfortable. You go through stages where you feel differently about it. Maria told me that she had been in an earlier relationship with Sally, her roommate from Australia; Sally had also come over a few times and we knew that they went on holiday together, but we did not think at the time that they were together.

With regards to my friends Hanan and Shamim, this is how we met. I was at the Deloitte offices for an International Women's Day event, and by the time I arrived, there was only one seat left in the front row of the auditorium. I sat down and realised that I knew the person on the left, so I turned to the person to the right, and I said, 'Hi, I'm Ellie Patsalos, I'm a partner here; are you a guest or are you one of our clients, or one of us?' She said, 'No, I'm her partner,' and pointed to one of the speakers, who was Shamim. Shamim presented her new book, and it was excellent. We also had Linda Papadopoulos, a psychiatrist, as a guest speaker, a good friend of mine. After the presentations finished, we had cocktails and nibbles outside, and Hanan officially introduced me to Shamim. After that, we started seeing each other regularly for lunch. In fact, I introduced them to Maria before I knew Maria was gay – I said, 'Maria, I've met these amazing women!' When I met Hanan and Shamim for lunch, they gave me some copies of their work, the book and the movie *I Can't Think Straight*. I didn't know what it was about, so I said to Maria, 'Our DVD player is broken, but before I see them again, I must see the movie – can I watch it on yours?' I didn't know what it was all about, though I knew Hanan and Shamim were gay. I just knew I had to watch some of it, so I could talk about it when I next saw them. It turned out that Maria had seen it before, and she told me she was laughing while we were watching the movie. She was telling this story to Hanan and Shamim afterwards. We are still very close, and Maria and I appeared as extras in a scene of one of their recent films, *Despite the Falling Snow*. We feel like they are part of the family, and it's the same on both sides.

Gradually, I started telling people about Maria's sexuality. In 2013, Nicolas got engaged to his wife-to-be – also called Maria – and I had started telling our friends and some family, but there were still some members of the family who did not know. In the meantime, Maria had broken up with Alex before Nicolas's engagement, and we were discussing how to handle it with the rest of the family. The wedding would be in 2014, and Maria and I agreed that we would not complicate matters by telling the whole extended family at that time; we would wait until after Nicolas got married, and then tell them. Our feeling was that if someone found out, that would be fine, but we were not going to make a big deal out of it; I knew that eventually telling my sisters would be difficult. Nicolas told his wife-to-be, and she was very comfortable with it. I told my friend Maro, and some of my closest friends, before I told my sisters. In fact, I didn't tell my aunts and my older cousins until recently. When I talked to my sisters, it was quite funny, because I was a bit hesitant to tell them, but I thought I had to go through with it. I was sitting in my sister's house, my three sisters and myself, and I said, 'I have to tell you something. It's about Maria.'

They immediately said, 'Is she OK?'

And I said, 'Yes, health-wise, she is fine, but the thing is, Maria is gay.'

And they said, 'That's OK, that's fine, we love her, there is no problem.' I think they were too shocked, and they did not really want to discuss it any further. Like us, they did not really absorb it. And the next time I went to Cyprus and saw them, they said, 'Is Maria still gay?' Really!

Having said that, every time she broke up with someone, Philip would say, 'Well, maybe she will meet a boy now.' And I would say, 'Philip, for God's sake! It's not going to happen, so accept it!'

With Nicolas, the main concern that we had was because he was so nice and kind, he might end up with the wrong girl! Before he met his wife, the last girl he dated was a skinny Australian girl – who, as it turned out, had an eating disorder. He wanted me to meet her, and I said to him, 'I only want to meet her if you are serious. If she is not the one, I don't want to know, just like I said before.' Apparently, she came to our house with Nicolas once when I was travelling overseas, because he knew I would refuse to meet her. It so happened that Philip was at home with his mother at the same time, so they met her, but eventually she went back to Australia because her visa ran out.

After he broke up with her, two friends of ours, Yioda and Peter Ioannou, mentioned they knew a doctor in London who lived around the corner from us, a beautiful girl, so why not arrange a meeting with Nicolas? I told Nicolas, and he was fine with it. I arranged to meet her at Yioda and Peter's house, and Maria came too. She was a lovely girl; it was just that Nicolas did not hit it off with her – it was too soon after his breakup with his earlier girlfriend. As it happened, the girl had an English boyfriend whom her parents did not want her to marry, so they were desperate for her to meet a Cypriot boy. Apparently, the girl agreed to the meeting to pacify her parents and to her surprise she liked Nicolas and indeed our family. In the end, it worked out for the best that Nicolas wasn't interested; she eventually married her English boyfriend. There were girls that he met at weddings and other social gatherings, but none of them developed into a serious relationship.

A Funeral, an Engagement and a Wedding

Over the years, I saw my dad deteriorating; the hard work of his earlier years had caught up with him. He always cultivated the olive and carob trees and enjoyed visiting his fields over the weekend. Eventually, his knees gave way, and what happens with most older people happened to him – he fell, broke his hip, and after that he never really recovered. He could have persevered with walking if he had been prepared to use a Zimmer frame, but he didn't. He also refused to use a wheelchair and stopped going to church. That was the thing I found most surprising, because my dad was so religious. Even though he got to a point when he could not walk at all, there were many people in the village whose families took them to the church in their wheelchairs so they could listen to the service. But my dad never wanted to do that. He said, 'I am done going to church. I can listen to the church service on the radio.' Later, a couple of years before his death, he also stopped watching TV. Before that, he had some programmes he particularly liked, and he watched a lot of video cassettes with Christian messages and services from Constantinople and other beautiful Orthodox churches around the world, but he stopped all that too. He had the radio next to him and he listened to the news, and that was it. I found all of it very odd.

I visited him a few times a year and he stayed in our family home. My sister Youla, the oldest daughter, lived close by and she was looking after Dad, especially after her husband Savvas died of Alzheimer's and she had more time to devote to him. My other sisters, Miroula and Elli, who live very close to our family home, were also looking after my dad, so he had excellent help.

I was glad that we were all there the summer he died. It was August 2010 and the whole family was in Cyprus on holiday. One morning, we planned to visit the Troodos mountains. My dad wasn't very well, so before we took off, we went to see him in the morning. He was weak, but he recognised us, and he looked fine. Then in the evening we were told he had deteriorated. That was Saturday, and on Sunday he died. I was glad I had spent a lot of time with him a few days before, and that we sat and talked and laughed. My brother, Takis, came back from England for the funeral, and it was an upbeat funeral. My dad was very well known in the village and a very funny person. He would always tell jokes, always had a twinkle in his eye and was always teasing the youngsters in the family.

After the funeral we came home, and we were recalling his jokes and lots of stories about him, celebrating his life. He had a great life. He built up a business from nothing and had seven lovely children, all successful, and lived to see them get married and give him grandchildren and great-grandchildren. He accumulated a lot of property due to hard work, even though he and my mum did not get anything from their parents, because their parents were not wealthy.

In September 2011, we went to Cyprus for a holiday. While we were there, Philip said to Maria and Nicolas, 'You always go out with your usual cousins, Xenios and Michalis. Why not go out with some of your other cousins for a change, Eliana, Stavros and Marina? Just to see some other kind of *parea* (group of friends).' They agreed to go out, and that night we had dinner with friends from Nicosia, who visited us in Larnaca. We had eaten, and their cousins, who had a family event, were running a bit late; it was midnight! We were returning to London the following day, and Maria said, 'It's very late, I don't feel like going out. Perhaps on our next visit to Cyprus!' Nicolas, being the nice guy and gentleman as always, said he would go because even though it was late, their cousins were very keen to meet up, and he did not want to let them down. Thus, Nicolas went out on his own with his cousins, and in one of the clubs that they went to in Larnaca, from a distance he saw Maria, his future wife. Maria came over to say hello to the group, because her roommate at university in Athens, Eliana, who was also studying law, was related to the gathered group that Nicolas was with. Maria had just finished her law degree and was on holiday in Cyprus visiting her parents in Nicosia. After her visit to Cyprus, she planned to go to England to do her master's degree in law. Eliana was still in Athens because she had one subject she had to retake, and she was there studying. Because of the connection with Eliana (who eventually became her maid of honour), she stopped by to say hello to Stavros and his sister Marina, and Nicolas was there. She said hello to Nicolas, and Marina said, 'Maria's going to London to do her masters,' so Nicolas said, 'Oh, we have to keep in touch when you are in London.' It was meant to be because she was coming to London for a year. They met just before that, and if Nicolas had not gone that night, they would not have met. The following morning, while sunbathing, Nicolas said to Philip, 'Dad, I met somebody I really liked. I think she's it.' From the first time he saw her, he felt that she was the one! It's amazing, how it happens.

That was in September. Maria came to London later that year in October, started her course, and on 18th January 2012, which was Nicolas's birthday, we met her for the first time. They had seen each other regularly since her arrival in London and Nicolas had shown us a picture of Maria on Facebook, so we knew what

A Funeral, an Engagement and a Wedding

she looked like. On 18th January, they were ready to meet us together and they were both very nervous. They went to a bar beforehand, and they had a drink or two for courage. Dinner was at Nobu in Mayfair opposite the May Fair Hotel. Maria was very polite; she didn't say much but she smiled; we liked her, and the main thing I remember is that she was tall, because Nicolas is so tall, he needed a tall girl! Later that year, in April 2012, our good friend Mike Geoghegan and his wife Jania invited us to visit their house in Barbados. It was Philip's sixtieth birthday, which as usual fell around Easter time, and so we went to Barbados and Maria joined us there as Nicolas's girlfriend. We all had a great time together, and that was the point when we realised that they were getting serious. There was no doubt about it.

The problem was that Nicolas felt it was a little too early to propose, because Maria had finished her studies in July, and she was going back to Cyprus. We were trying to determine what he would do, and how he might approach it. He said, 'I'm not really ready yet,' and so Maria went back to Cyprus in July. Nicolas was planning to go to Cyprus in late summer, take Maria on holiday to Istanbul and propose. He bought a beautiful ring, and he was calling her to tell her that he was coming to Cyprus and about the holiday that he had planned – but Maria told him that she had accepted a job with a Cyprus law firm, one of the top law firms in Nicosia. Nicolas was very upset because he felt that if she got a job, she would probably not come to England later. Eventually he went to Cyprus in September, they went on holiday to Istanbul, and he proposed – there was a bit of a hoo-ha about the ring, and she realised something was happening because he was trying to make sure that the ring wasn't inspected when going through Istanbul customs. At the hotel Nicolas enquired as to whether there was a safe in the hotel; apparently there was a standing joke that if a man asked whether there was a safe in the room, then it meant there was a ring! We were anxiously waiting for the call from Nicolas, confirming the engagement; the call came through, they both came back to Cyprus and the two families had a dinner together to celebrate.

The question now was, when would Maria come back to London? She was already working, so they agreed that she would stay for a few more months and then would resign and inform her firm that she was engaged and was moving to London. That was on 9th September 2012, and then on 26th January 2013 she moved to London, and they were engaged in the summer, with an official engagement party at Coworth Park on 4th August. We had already decided that the wedding would be in Cyprus, so we felt that for people who could not come to Cyprus for whatever reason, the following year we would have an engagement party in London to celebrate.

We were originally told about the venue by our friends Jasminder and Amrit Singh, whom we'd met through Mike Geoghegan. They lived in Ascot, and when we said we were planning the engagement party, they told us that Coworth Park was the place to book. They had their son's engagement party there and it was apparently amazing! We looked at a couple of other venues, but Coworth Park was by far the best. When Maria came to visit, we visited the hotel, she loved it and we booked it. It was the most fabulous party – we had a marquee in the grounds, with a harpist playing music, and we were very lucky with the excellent weather. The champagne reception took place outside on the beautiful, manicured lawn. The whole immediate family from Cyprus came; we had fifteen people staying with us in our house. Every room was occupied. It was an amazing event, even more so than a wedding. The Sunday after the party, Prince Harry and Prince William were playing polo nearby, so there was a lot of police and security there. Coworth Park Hotel has stables, and it is a truly English country hotel. The food and service were excellent, and the rooms spectacular: Nicolas and Maria got the bridal suite; we had a beautiful cottage, just Philip and I and my three sisters, and our daughter Maria and some of her friends. At the time, Maria was very upset because she had just broken up with her then-partner, but she brought some university friends with her and Nicolas knew them as well. It was a very successful event.

The following year, in 2014, there was the wedding in Cyprus, and then there was my retirement, so I had so many events, six retirement parties that year before I left in December! We had the wedding to organise in Cyprus, and the hen party in Athens. Maria organised the hen party in July 2014 with Eliana since they had lived in Athens together for many years during their studies. We had dinners, and then the bouzouki, the live music, and I danced, though I ended up having a problem with my back; Saturday night was the last night and on Sunday we were leaving. On Sunday morning, I was in so much pain I could not move my hand at all! I had to call one of my partners at Deloitte in Athens to get me a doctor in a private hospital. I had to go and get a cortisone injection because I was in unbearable pain and needed strong painkillers. When I returned to London, I had an MRI scan of my shoulder but thankfully it was just a tear; nothing was broken. We still had a blast! My friends Maro and Egly from Cyprus joined us; my daughter Maria came with Laura, her girlfriend at the time, and Maria's mum came with a friend of hers. Initially, I said to Maria, 'You do whatever you want, party with your friends, we don't have to come,' but she wanted me and her mother there, and her sister Evi also came; she was in Greece on holiday with her family, so she joined us for a day. When Maria went to Cyprus in September, she had another get-together with her friends – still, the main event was in Athens, so it was nice to be part of that.

The wedding was magical. So much organisation, and of course there were a lot of agonising days deciding where the wedding would take place in Cyprus. Nicolas and Maria wanted to have their wedding by the sea. We identified a venue which was by the sea but had no infrastructure. The initial idea was to create the decking and the kitchen and other infrastructure; however, it proved difficult to accommodate a sit-down dinner for three hundred people with a waiter service, and it was ridiculously expensive. In the end it was unanimously agreed to have the wedding at the Anassa Hotel in Paphos, the best five-star hotel in Cyprus, located by the beach. We were in a dilemma, because after the financial crisis in Cyprus in 2013, people were more conservative about spending money, but I did not want to compromise on my standards for my son's wedding, and Maria was caught up in the middle with Nicolas. Another logistical factor was the fact that the Anassa was a long way away from Nicosia, where all of Maria's family and friends were based. Her parents were very keen to invite a large number of friends and family whom we couldn't invite to the wedding ceremony due to the restriction in the overall number. Therefore, we agreed that we would also have an additional wedding reception in Nicosia so we could invite a wider selection of family and friends. Eventually, we came to an agreement and Maria's parents hosted the reception in Nicosia at the Hilton Park Hotel.

Because the photographer and the videographers who covered the engagement event at Coworth Park were amazing, we arranged for them to come to Cyprus. It was the first wedding in Cyprus where they had photographs taken by drones. That's why some of the wedding photos are so amazing. It was a magical night with lots of fun and dancing! We had a large number of international guests from the UK, the US, Australia, Barbados, Colombia and so on. All Nicolas and Maria's friends joined us, and they combined the wedding celebration with a summer holiday! Many guests attended both receptions. We organised a coach to take them from the Anassa to the Hilton Park Hotel in Nicosia and to bring them back to the Anassa.

We went back to our home in Larnaca on Saturday (the wedding was on Thursday 11th September) because another friend's son was getting married in Ayia Napa on Saturday 13th September – yet another wedding! And we had to recover so we could be ready for the second wedding reception on Sunday 14th September in Nicosia. Since Maria's parents were hosting this reception, they were more involved in the details compared to us, but we still all had the food tasting, decided on the drinks, the decorations, the flowers and other details. On Sunday late morning we arrived at the Hilton Park Hotel, and we were ready for the reception, which started at 6:00pm. We had over five hundred guests for drinks and canapes, and it was very successful. Around midnight, we went to another more intimate venue, with plenty more drinks and finger food, where the youngsters danced until the early hours of Monday. Overall, another excellent celebration!

Six Retirement Parties

All the partners at Deloitte UK know that sixty is the year of retirement. There are no exceptions. In fact, every couple of years, the board reviewed this partnership clause, and all board members (having taken soundings from various partners) agreed that sixty should remain the retirement age. In other firms within Deloitte, the age of retirement ranged from fifty-five to sixty-five. In the US, for example, the retirement age is sixty-two; in Cyprus, sixty-five; and in Germany, fifty-five – but there is a guideline from the global firm that retirement age falls somewhere between fifty-five and sixty-five. By 2013, I was starting to get very anxious that I only had one year remaining of my tenure at Deloitte.

I was used to Deloitte having full control of my life. They looked after my secretarial support, travel, health, life insurance and so on; they made sure that all these issues were taken care of, so our focus would be on our clients, our staff and bringing in revenue. Even though the deadline was fast approaching, it was very easy to live in denial because I was so busy and doing so many things that I never got time to step back. 2014 was a very big year for me because it was my sixtieth birthday in May, we had Nicolas's wedding in September and my retirement at the end of December. Still, it really got to me – how could I survive, not being part of the Deloitte family that I had known for close to thirty years?

I knew that when I retired Deloitte wanted me to keep a working relationship with them in some capacity, though at the time I was not sure what that would be. Before the wedding in Cyprus in September, we agreed that I needed some more time to fully transition my Bloomberg LCSP role to a couple of Deloitte partners. It made sense to continue working with Deloitte to ensure the transition was smoothly executed, so I set up my own personal company and worked with them as a consultant, but nothing else changed. This arrangement did not prohibit me from taking on another consulting role. Closer to the end of 2014, I continued discussions with Martin Geller and Peter Grauer, who was, and still is, chairman of Bloomberg LP, about a future role with either firm, since it was always assumed that I would do so after my retirement. We agreed that it would be best for my role to be with Geller, supporting Bloomberg; Geller and Co. provides a huge level of services to Bloomberg. By late 2014, I had a commitment from Martin that I would start working with them in New York from January 2015.

In late spring 2014, during one of our meetings with another client, Wargaming, I mentioned to them that I was retiring later that year, and they were very keen to see whether I could consider working with them as an advisor. Wargaming is a global online gaming company based and headquartered in Cyprus. I was also their Global Lead Tax Partner, assisted by Martin Rowley, who is a US corporate tax partner, and we provided tax services to them. The company was an audit and tax client for the Deloitte Cyprus firm and through Christis Christoforou, the Global LCSP, I was introduced to them to assist them with some US-specific tax issues. They were very happy with the work we carried out for them on a couple of tricky issues, and when they heard I was retiring, they said to me, 'Could you come and be our global advisor, and set up a tax department, because we need someone with your expertise to help us?' I thought, 'Why not?' It seemed like a good opportunity for me, because of course I am Cypriot, and I have a house there. Since I agreed with Deloitte that while I was working with them, I could accept other roles, I agreed to start my contract with Wargaming on 1st October. I set up my own company, Patsalos Consulting, in late September 2014, and Deloitte helped me with that process. I sent my first invoice to Deloitte and Wargaming in October of that year, after Nicolas's wedding. I had still not transitioned the Bloomberg relationship to another partner because there was so much to do, and Bloomberg and Geller were involved in the process of identifying my successor(s). It wasn't easy to find one person to replace me because I had been involved for thirty years, so we agreed that we would have two or three partners in different roles, which is what we eventually implemented.

Because of my global pattern of travelling over the years, I started having my retirement parties and dinners early in 2014. I had six parties in total, so wherever I went for my last conference or regional trip, I had a celebration! I started with Latin America because I always went there in February, which is summer, for my annual visit. I went to Buenos Aires, Sao Paulo and Mexico City. I had a lovely time at one of my favourite tango shows and dinner in Buenos Aires with the partners I worked with over the years. In Sao Paulo we had an enjoyable lunch with the Deloitte and Bloomberg teams to say adios! In Mexico City, they took me to a private members' club for lunch with all the partners and the staff who worked with me, and they invited some of the Bloomberg people from Brazil and Mexico, so it was a combined party. In April, I travelled to Asia for our annual conference. I visited Tokyo, China, Hong Kong and Singapore. I had big parties in Hong Kong and Singapore, where the conference was, and in Japan I went out with my Deloitte team, plus some people from Bloomberg and HSBC.

The big event was in London on 12th November 2014 at the May Fair Hotel, which is owned by our friends, the Singh family.

In total, I had three events in London. One was the November client event, which was the key party that I invited my top clients to, for example the senior executives from HSBC. I also invited some of my retired clients whom I worked with before their retirement and continued to stay in touch with, plus some of my global partners from the US, Asia, Cyprus and Greece, and the Deloitte non-executive directors from the UK board. In addition, I invited some retired partners, such as Peter Shawyer, who had been my mentor. I invited Nigel Davy, who was with me at the beginning at Spicer & Pegler when he was Head of Tax for the law firms and professional firms; I learned so much from him. Some of my clients could not attend because they were overseas, such as Mike Geoghegan, former Group CEO of HSBC, who is still a close friend.

For the main event with all my clients and senior Deloitte partners, I had my family with me: Philip and the kids, but also some of my family from Cyprus, including my nephew Xenakis Kalli and his wife Miranda, and some close family friends based in London. I'd prepared for my speech that night for a long time, so I knew everything by heart; I did not want any notes. I talked about my family and all the things we had gone through over the years and thanked my clients and my colleagues for their support. Our global chairman gave a glowing introduction about me and my long career with Deloitte. It was a fantastic and emotional evening!

I also had a party for the rest of the firm, with the partners, senior managers and directors who'd worked with me over the years at Sketch, a venue in Central London, and another party for my expatriate tax group. The partners of my group organised a lovely dinner for me at an iconic restaurant in London, Scott's. Later that year, we had our annual Global Tax conference and during the presentation of a tribute to me, they organised a video recording from Chris Harvey, the Global Head of Financial

Services, and the Global LCSP for HSBC who replaced me on that account, which was excellent. He was very complimentary! Over the years I had mentored and helped many partners, primarily partners in my tax group and in my service client teams. Before Chris, the GFSI Leader was Jack Ribeiro, a great partner who was very successful in that role, a big personality and a huge fan of mine. Another of my mentees was Guy Seeger, who worked closely with me on the Bloomberg account and became the Bloomberg GLCSP after I retired.

It was a very emotional time, receiving all these accolades from the people I had worked with. But oh my God, 2014 was a year of choosing from menus, champagne and canapes, wine and food, because we had so many events – and of course that was the year we had the wedding! All these parties – by the end of that year, I never wanted to think about parties again!

My last retirement party was in New York in late November, after the party in London. All my US colleagues, Bloomberg and Geller wanted to honour me, and at the time, Mike Bloomberg was still mayor of New York. I invited him, and it was very exciting that he accepted. His security people arrived first to ensure that it was safe for him to attend. My friend Marigay McKee was also there with Bill Ford, her fiancé. Peter Grauer, Martin Geller, Deloitte colleagues and Marigay all spoke, thanking me for my services and friendship. Finally, while I was in New York, I organised a private dinner for some people who were very close to me, including partners from Deloitte in the US, Daniel McCarthy, formerly at Bloomberg, and Philip Halliday at Credit Suisse. Philip, my husband, accompanied me to both events, and that really finished off the retirement party phase of 2014.

While these events were all amazing, inside I was still traumatised. I had nightmares and I couldn't sleep at night, I was very worried, and I didn't know how my life would be and how it would feel after I left Deloitte. Even though I had two external roles already in motion, I was still very upset about severing my Deloitte links. In fact, Deloitte offered me the option to continue my consulting role after 2014, but after reflecting on it, I decided that it was time to cut those ties. The longer I stayed semi-connected, but not fully, the worse I would feel. Even the secretaries, the receptionist, the security guards and the people in the adjacent coffee shop told me they would miss me, because I was somebody everybody knew – my presence, my character and the way I dressed. In fact, just two weeks earlier, I had been at Deloitte with the charity Breast Cancer Now and another partner, Siara Hewitt, who supports the Women's Network, said to me, 'Oh Ellie, I remember you when you were a partner, coming down to see Ian Hook,' – whom she was working for at the time – 'with your beautiful dresses and high heels, I always looked forward to seeing you.' She said she was always wondering what I would be wearing when I was coming over to a meeting with Ian. She said she always looked up to me, and the way I dressed helped her realise that you could be a partner and dress nicely rather than in the drab black colours people usually wore. I felt so good to hear that young female partners have benefited from my presence while at Deloitte.

On 29th December, I arranged with my PA to accompany me as I entered the Deloitte building as a partner for the last time. I brought my PC, my iPad, my phone, my badge – I had to hand it all in. I got to keep my phone number, but everything else had to change. While I was still a Deloitte consultant, I could freely enter and leave the office – I had a different-coloured badge. It was so sad, and I felt very aware that from that day forward, when I had to visit Deloitte, it would be as a guest.

Skydiving

In recent years I have put more of my efforts into supporting charities I care about. I support a medical charity, an art charity and a humanitarian child development charity, which is a perfect combination for me!

The first charity I became involved with is Breast Cancer Now. When I was first introduced to it by my good friend Marigay McKee, the charity was called Breakthrough Breast Cancer. There were many breast cancer charities then, but Breakthrough was one of the only charities that devoted all the money they raised to research; they use the money to maintain a scientific centre in South London, where they have specialist scientists looking at all kinds of different ways to stop the metastasis of breast cancer. In fact, they identified the BRCA mutation, so now women can see if they test positive for the BRCA-1 or BRCA-2 gene mutations.

I was introduced to Marigay McKee by Mike Geoghegan, the group CEO of HSBC. He met her at an event to support young people who were being assisted by corporations to get into higher education. At the time, Marigay was the chief merchant at Harrods and a board member. Mohamed Al-Fayed, the CEO of Harrods, was expected to be there, but he could not make it that day so Marigay attended instead. She happened to sit next to Mike Geoghegan, who had worked for years in Latin America before returning to the UK, so he spoke Spanish – and Marigay is half-Spanish. They started up a conversation in both Spanish and English and got on very well.

Afterwards, Mike said to me, 'Ellie, I met this amazing woman – she's just like you! She is clever, good-looking and very outgoing. She told me that she was late filing her tax return, and I said, "Well, you have to meet Ellie, she is the best tax person I know – she takes care of all my tax affairs, and I think you two will really hit it off."'

At first, the three of us tried to meet as a group, but our travelling schedules made it impossible. Eventually, I said to Mike, 'Forget it – I will contact Marigay and arrange for the two of us to meet, and then later when you are available to join us, we can have another dinner.' Marigay and I went to lunch at the Cipriani, and it was love at first sight – on the friendship side! She was a lovely woman and we had so much in common even though I am ten years older than her, including our star signs – both Geminis! She was going through a tough divorce with her husband and having two children involved wasn't easy. In my opinion, she was too nice to him and paid much more than she should because she was very keen to ensure that the children stayed close to their father, which I agree is a very good principle. She was not only clever but very beautiful and a loyal friend.

When we first met, Marigay told me about the Breakthrough Breast Cancer Charity and that she was doing a skydive to raise money for them. At the time it would have been too late for me to do the jump with her, but I was very tempted by the idea. It was something I had always wanted to do for as long as I could remember. For years, at Christmases and birthdays, I had been asking Philip and the kids to get me such a present for my birthday, but Philip always thought that was very dangerous. I always dreamed, as a young woman, that I was flying, and it was such a liberating feeling.

That was the first time I heard about Breakthrough, and because of my condition and the family history, I was very aware of how important it is to continue to maintain the scientific research that they were supporting, so a year later, I did the skydive for Breakthrough. Marigay introduced me to the charity and then I introduced Maria, and that's how it all started. We had to raise twenty-five thousand pounds, and they took care of everything else: the gear, the aircraft and the instructor. Philip drove us to a small aerospace outside Oxford, and I jumped out of the plane. I raised over fifty thousand pounds with that skydive because it was a very difficult challenge and not many people were up to it! The only time I was slightly scared was when the time came to tumble out of the plane. It was like having to take vaccinations as a child; I had to go first.

I was up there with six couples. Each volunteer was strapped to, and accompanied by, a RAF pilot. A cameraman jumped out before us, so he could film us going down. We edged towards the front of the plane which had no doors and just tumbled over – it took a few seconds, and then we turned in the air, made sure that our hands and feet were in the right position, smiled at the camera, and then the parachute opened. We then glided along, and we landed. We had to make sure that our knees were bent backwards just before we landed, otherwise we might break a leg. The whole process doesn't take more than five minutes, and it was just the most amazing experience. When it was over, I was ready to go back up there again! I had no fear whatsoever – Maria my daughter did the jump a year later, and she also enjoyed it, although she had a bad experience when she landed, but I loved it. We had a debrief after the jump where they asked us questions about it, and I said, 'What's not to like? One is strapped to a RAF pilot, a real hunk!' These pilots participated in such activities for extra money, and they were really good-looking guys!

That was the first time I met members of the charity, and they realised I was very committed, so we did a lot of events together over the years. I attended a lot of their functions, and I went to the scientific centre to learn more about what they do. I invited the team from the charity to come to Deloitte and do a number of presentations to female partners and to our Women's Network, which helped to raise the awareness of breast cancer screening, early detection and prevention through proper diet and exercise. I also attended their presentations at various City women's organisations, for example on International Women's Day in Coutts Bank. We started discussing the possibility of inviting me to be a member of the board, but at the same time, they started looking at merging with another Breast Cancer charity. This was a positive move, as I was always saying to them, 'Why are there so many different breast cancer charities? If you merge with another, you have more impact, and you have more opportunity to grow quickly.' But there are always politics, even in the charity sector.

When Breakthrough Breast Cancer merged with Breast Cancer Campaign and became Breast Cancer Now (BCN), most of our contacts left so we had to work with new teams. There were discussions again as to whether I should be considered as board member and I met a few of the board members. It was quite a positive experience – the chairwoman was very good and the CEO was nice – but I decided it would be better to wait until the merger was consolidated. We agreed that I would continue to stay close to them and do more fundraising, for example leading the Kilimanjaro challenge in 2016, where thirteen brave women joined the group and collectively raised more than £200,000.

The second charity I became involved with was more of a surprise. When we were on holiday in New Zealand in February 2016, I got a call from a recruitment company on behalf of British Youth Opera. They told me that they were looking for a senior executive with a financial background and links to the corporate world. They asked me if I was interested in joining their board. At the time, I was considering a board position at Breast Cancer Now and since that didn't come through, I thought, why not? I am not a fanatical opera lover, but I like opera very much, and I knew that I would enjoy helping young people to progress in their careers. Either way, I had nothing to lose and so I wrote a nice letter to British Youth Opera about why I was right for the job. I mentioned my involvement with the Royal Opera House through the Deloitte Ignite partnership and my financial and City background. In late March 2016 I went for an interview with the chairman and a couple of board members. They really liked me and offered me the role. I accepted and started in April 2016.

British Youth Opera is a leading UK opera training company and arts charity. Its key objective is to discover, develop and launch the next generation of opera professionals. It provides professional performance, rehearsals, workshops and production opportunities for emerging singers, production trainees and instrumentalists on the threshold of their careers. The annual summer season (which starts in early September, before the Royal Opera season in mid-September begins) produces two operas. I went to the 2017 rehearsals and it was an amazing experience, seeing the young singers perform. I watched both operas, *The Vanishing Bridegroom* and *Don Giovanni*. In September, I invited twenty of my friends who like opera and we attended the *Don Giovanni* performance at the Peacock Theatre, which is located very close to the LSE in Holborn. It was a very memorable experience! In November 2017, I attended their gala dinner and I invited some of my friends who are opera lovers and also great philanthropists, so they supported the charity. One of the auction prizes I bid for was a behind-the-scenes tour of the Windsor Royal Estate. On 4th May 2018, we went for the tour, and it was an amazing experience. We were very lucky that the weather was perfect, sunny and hot, so it made the royal gardens look even more beautiful with all their fantastic colours. With the Royal Wedding of Prince Harry and Meghan so close, it was a fascinating visit!

Finally, the third charity I support, the Madrinha Trust, was set up by Mike and Jania Geoghegan. Mike donated the funds and Jania is actively involved as the chairman of the charity. The good thing about establishing a funded charitable trust is that you don't have to fundraise. You have the money, and you spend it, bearing in mind the objectives and goals of the trust. The objectives of the charity are the advancement of education and the relief of poverty through the provision of funds to educational and other projects anywhere in the world, but in particular Africa and the developing world. The charity's vision is to develop future leaders of the developing world. It provides access to education for young, clever and ambitious students to progress to tertiary education.

Before the approval of any financial support, the mentees must agree to participate in the mentoring process. We currently have approval for sixty-three mentees in eleven countries. Before we agree to accept a student's application, they must complete an essay based on subjects we provide and undertake an interview with a member of the Education and Mentoring (E&M) committee. As a member of the E&M committee, I conduct interviews – and I love that because I really enjoy speaking to the young applicants. Each successful student is allocated a mentor, whose role is to support, guide and assist the mentee in the academic, personal and general development aspects of their lives. The mentors are experienced professionals, and we try to match them with the mentees, so they have the same subject matter expertise. What we expect from the mentees is that they go on to contribute to their local community. For example, if they study to be doctors, we ask that they practice locally or assist a local medical practice. We support a lot of teachers, and we recently found out that in Ghana, some of the teachers were not being paid by the government, because the country was in a mess, and they had no money. The Madrinha Trust paid their salaries to enable them to meet their daily needs. Now they are being paid, and they are so grateful. They teach in the communities that they started out in themselves, and that's what we want to do, to get the young people to develop and continue to be involved in their community. I am a mentor for three girls in South Africa, each one of them different. One of them is a medical student and she is a real star, so hard-working – her average grade is something like ninety-five out of a hundred. These kids come from broken families. Sometimes their dads moved away when they were very young, or both of their parents died, and they live with their grandparents. They live in challenging conditions. It is really very sad, but they are very conscientious and study hard because they want to get on and have better lives.

Climbing Mountains

On 25th September 2016, we left London for Arusha to start our new adventure, climbing Kilimanjaro to raise funds for breast cancer research. I organised it because I had always wanted to do the Kilimanjaro climb, but before that, in November 2013, the opportunity came up to go to Nepal and trek towards the base camp in Everest. My friend Marigay McKee knew someone, Dave Meckin, who, in addition to his day job as a lecturer in financial matters, had a passion for adventures and organised several excursions, including trekking in Nepal. We decided not to undertake this adventure for the benefit of any charity since it was planned for a few months after the skydive and we did not feel it was right to be asking the same people for money so soon afterwards; therefore we just did it as a personal adventure.

There were six of us, including me and Marigay; my daughter Maria; Martin, who worked with Marigay at Harrods; and Jason, a friend of Marigay's. We arrived in Kathmandu on 3rd November during the Festival of Lights, so the city was glowing and sparkling with all the lights everywhere! We stayed at one of the best hotels in Kathmandu which was, by Western standards, a three-star hotel. Dave kept telling us that this was the most luxurious place we would have for the next week when we would be trekking towards Everest. The following morning, very excited, we took off from the local airport in a small plane and headed to Lukla, a very small town from where all the trekkers started their climb. Lukla has the unique reputation of having the shortest runway in the whole world, so we all prayed that the pilot was an experienced one who would be able to stop before the plane hit the mountain!

All went well, and after a brief stop to have lunch at the local 'tea house' we started the trek. All trekkers take the same route towards the Everest base camp. Our plan was to go across from the base camp towards Tengboche so we could have better views of the mountain, rather than go to the foot of Everest. We passed the Dudh Kosi valley en route to Monjo, the gateway to the Sagarmatha National Park. We went across many bridges, accompanied by the shepherds and the colourful and scary bulls which were carrying all our belongings on their backs, and on to Namche Bazaar, a relatively big town where Marigay and I managed to get a hair appointment and a massage. We had so much fun that day. From there we continued our upward trek until at last we saw the majestic view of Everest, 8,848 metres. It was breathtaking!

We managed to get up to the Everest View Hotel with its magnificent views. This hotel had a long history; it was built years before by Japanese businessmen who were planning to fly their guests all the way up there directly from Lukla. However, they didn't calculate the risk of altitude sickness! Their first guests almost died from the sudden ascent and for years the hotel was closed. Now it has reopened and is used by trekkers taking a break during their adventure. Dave was very experienced, so he kept taking us uphill and then downhill, so we got acclimatised to the altitude. Apart from Maria, who was unwell at the beginning of our travels, we were all fine in that respect.

After seven days on the road, we reached Tengboche, 3,875 metres up. That evening we went for evening prayers at the Tengboche monastery. The following day, our last before our descent, we walked past Pangboche and exceeded four thousand metres before we headed back down to Tengboche. That was the toughest day, because we went so high and then had to return to our original starting point; another four hours of trekking! By the time we were close to our hotel it was quite late and very dark, so we had to use our head torches to see where we were going.

Marigay said to me, 'I can't imagine going back in the same route towards Lukla and staying overnight there for our last night. That tea house smelled of shit and urine.'

I agreed with her. 'That night is 10th November, Maria's birthday. Not looking forward to it at all!'

Marigay said, 'I wonder whether we could fly down to Lukla by helicopter?'

I replied, 'Let's check it out, and if it's possible, I'm in!'

When we asked the head shepherd, he just laughed; he thought we were joking. We told him we were dead serious and asked him to check if a helicopter could take us down the following morning and how much it would cost. When he realised that we were serious, he checked it out and told us that yes, we could use a helicopter to go down. It would only take forty-five minutes and cost $10,000. We jumped for joy and so the following morning we flew to Lukla. Marigay and I agreed to split the cost. Some of the shepherds, who had never flown in a helicopter, joined us and they were ecstatic!

The whole experience was quite tough, and we were sleeping in some rough conditions, but it was nothing compared to Kilimanjaro. We slept in the teahouses, which had no central heating and no showers and smelled badly! Wherever we were staying, the toilet was outside, it was bitterly cold and sometimes the rooms had ice inside – but at least we were sleeping in a room, compared to a tent where you cannot even stand up. The food we ate every day was the traditional dal bhat with lentils, very helpful for energy, with no fried food or alcoholic drinks allowed. Our excursion in Nepal was the first time we'd done this kind of trail adventure, and we just loved it. When we got back to London, we were all excited about what we had just experienced.

When we got back, Maria said, 'I think we should forget about Kilimanjaro. We are told that it is not as scenic as Everest and much harder! We got a glimpse of what it's about, let's not do it.'

I said, 'Fine.'

Then, a few months later, we were talking to some people about Everest and saying what a great experience it was. Afterwards, Maria and I were in the car, and I said, 'Maria, I think we must go ahead and do Kilimanjaro. We said we were going to, so let's go for it.'

She said, 'You're right, Mum. Besides, we still have some of the gear. We might as well use it again!'

I contacted Marigay, who had since moved to New York. I said, 'Marigay, are you in?' and she said, 'Yes, I'm in!'

Marigay invited some women from her circle of friends in New York, and I invited women from mine, including some women from the company I worked for in Cyprus. In the end, we had fifteen women – a couple dropped out towards the very end, but it was still a good number, thirteen. As I was the leader of the gang, I contacted the breast cancer charity, and through the charity, we approached a couple of travel companies. We decided on the one that Deloitte had used for a similar adventure when the partners and staff did the Kilimanjaro climb for our chosen charities, and we were off!

We started planning this in autumn 2015 for the same time the following year. September 2016 was the date of the adventure, and it seemed a long way off at first, but just like my recent trip to Antarctica, it came around surprisingly quickly. The charity paid all our expenses, and we agreed to raise a minimum of ten thousand pounds – actually, it was meant to be five thousand pounds or more each, but in order to subsidise those who weren't able to raise that much, we had set a minimum of ten thousand for some of the businesswomen in the group. I raised close to fifty thousand, and eventually we raised over two hundred thousand pounds between us.

We knew it was going to be a very tough adventure, and the preparation was all very exciting but also quite fearful. In Everest, it was flat and hilly, but this time it was much, much steeper! We started at the foot of the mountain and then, as we climbed up and down, it was not just the height but the altitude and lack of oxygen we would need to worry about. To prepare for the climb, a group of us met in Central London and walked for six to eight hours together, choosing hilly neighbourhoods. I supplemented those walks by walking on my own, and at the gym my trainer devised special exercises for me to help me with endurance. Maria and I went for a weekend in the Peak District and had a guide who took us up three peaks over a weekend. We knew it was a similar terrain to Kilimanjaro, which was very helpful – and very tiring! With the Cypriot girls we also trained a few weekends in Cyprus (Maria joined us for one weekend) up in Troodos Mountains and followed some tough trails! The group included the UK team: Maria and I; Becky from the BCN charity; Avril, a friend of BCN; Gabriella Piccini and Susanne Given, friends of Marigay. The Cyprus contingent included Nasia Hadjivasili and Marianna Pantelidou, who worked with me at Wargaming in Cyprus, and Christina O'Neill (a friend of Marianna, also from Cyprus). The US contingent included Marigay, Deirdre Quinn and her sister Paula Sewell, and Susan Harrison (Marigay's friend's daughter-in-law, who was based in New York). I met all the team members in London and in New York, so we all bonded before the adventure! We also had a female doctor from London who accompanied us throughout the climb.

When we arrived in Arusha and talked to other groups who had completed the climb, we realised we had a problem. We were following the Rongai Route starting from the Nalemoru Gate

(1,950 metres), and the plan was to reach the summit (5,895 metres) in five days. The travel agency had misled us about the amount of time we needed to climb Kilimanjaro without getting into difficulties with altitude sickness. Maria questioned it early on, and then I went back to them and said, 'Five days is not a lot of time to climb all the way up. People do it in a minimum of six or seven days, so why did you not advise us to go for the longer option?'

They said, 'The charities always offer this option.' But our charity didn't know, since this was the first Kilimanjaro trip they had sponsored, and we were all relying on the travel company to give us this advice and information, not the charity! Because of that, a few of us did not make it all the way to the top and I was one of them!

Funnily enough, when we went to Nepal, Maria had more of a problem with the altitude sickness. I didn't, but in Kilimanjaro, it was the other way around. During the first day we trekked through farmer fields and the forest zone, and we stayed at Simba Camp (2,600 metres). On day two, we left the camp and climbed through the moorland. As we climbed, the trees became less and less and then disappeared. After nine hours of trekking, we reached our next campsite, Kikelewa Cave (3,678 metres). Day three, we started trekking a steeper trek to Mawenzi Tarn Hut (4,295 metres). In the afternoon, we took a short circular acclimatisation walk to a higher altitude to help us the following day when we would be trekking at much higher terrain. On day four, we trekked six hours to the base camp, Kibo (4,700 metres). I remember very well the shortness of breath and the constant sickness I suffered from the time we left Kikelewa Cave. Maria was next to me, encouraging me to keep going. We had a memorable photo in front of Kibo Camp sign, and I look totally washed out and pure white. Upon arrival at Kibo Camp, we were told we had to rest and prepare for the summit night. Overall, it was a great experience up to a certain altitude, around 3,500 metres. That was when I started feeling unwell. I couldn't keep anything down and was just being sick all the time. The doctor told me that I had to try to eat anyway because even if I ate and was sick immediately afterwards, some of it would still stay in my system. I would eat, and then as soon as I had finished eating, I would go outside and throw up again. People started timing me, counting from one to ten, and then everything would come back up. Looking back, it was quite funny, but at the time, I was getting very weak. Everyone knew that there was no way I could make it, but I could not accept defeat.

Descent

It was bitterly cold, and I was so unwell with little energy. I did not have a lot of strength left and was also suffering from lack of sleep in a tent where one could not properly stand up – we were always crouching to prepare for the day or to get ready for bed in the evenings. The sleeping mats came in bundles and we paid the shepherds five dollars every day to unwrap them and blow them out at night and then, in the mornings, to remove the air and wrap them up again. I just did not have the energy for any of that. The other thing was, as you get up so high, you have to keep drinking water, and the more we drank, the more we had to go to the bathroom – which meant leaving the tent, putting on boots and clothes, and going through that whole procedure. I was so drained I could not even do that. We had showers, and eventually I tried using one because I couldn't bear to go outside. It was not perfect, but in desperation, it was better than nothing!

I was sharing a tent with Marigay, and Maria was sharing with Nasia, who was working on my tax team in Cyprus. They became very good friends by the end of the climb. On summit night, day five, we had to wake up at eleven-thirty in the evening and have something to eat before we started walking for the top. When they woke us, I was so disorientated that I put Marigay's boots on by accident because I had got up before her and I thought the first boots I saw were mine. It was pitch black at the time.

Her boots are bigger than mine, but I was all right with them – she was wondering why her boots were tight and I said, 'Maybe because you are wearing three pairs of socks tonight!'

We went out and had something to eat. I had some dry toast, I was sick again as usual and then we started our final trek up to the top. The shepherds kept telling us, 'Go slow, *polepole*, one step in front of the other, get into a rhythm.' Despite not feeling at all well, when I looked up and saw that the other groups who camped on the same campsite already started in front of us, I must say that it was the most beautiful sight! Everyone had their head torches on, so they could see where they were walking, and they were walking one at a time along the path which was winding up and up the mountain as far as you could see! I was delighted that I was still participating since this was the final push. I still thought that somehow, I could make it!

That night was extremely long and challenging, with us walking up to sixteen hours. From Kibo Camp we had to walk to Gilman's Point (5,680 metres) on the rim of the volcanic crater for sunrise. We then had to continue across the snow around the rim for a further two to three hours or longer, depending on how much strength was left, for the final push to Uhuru Peak (5,895 metres) – Africa's highest point! And then it was the descent back to Gilman's Point and back down to Kibo base camp.

I was walking upwards for about two hours before I realised I could not continue. I stopped many times to rest and have some water with the shepherd looking after me close by. Maria stayed back to be with me and to make sure I was OK. She had a sudden nosebleed, which gave me even more time to sit and recover. Despite that, I needed to stop more and more. I was hallucinating, being sick again and unable to move. Once the doctor was notified, she came down and said to me, 'You must go straight down. Not even one foot further.' I was crying by then. I did not want to leave because I was the leader of the gang, I organised everything and I was the fittest I'd ever been. I didn't want to miss this crucial part! But I had no energy at all, so I agreed.

Once the decision was taken, I was so relieved, but I couldn't imagine that I would have two more hours of descent before I could lie down! I held the shepherd closely as he helped me down, and said, 'Thank goodness this nightmare is over.' I just wanted to be in my tent, I wanted to sleep, but I had to walk for another two hours to get back down and going down was even worse because it was so slippery, I was holding on for dear life.

Because the shepherd had to go back and join the rest of the group, they radioed the camp and someone else came up mid-way to take over and help me get down. They were all very acclimatised since they climbed the mountain twice per month at least! After what felt like ages, we arrived back at Kibo base camp and I was taken straight to my tent. I was given some tea and I was told to sleep for an hour. Afterwards they woke me up, and together with Gabriella (who was unwell much earlier than me and was already in her tent) we were given some more tea and dry toast so we had enough energy to walk down to the campsite below, a three- to four-hour trek depending on how quickly we could walk. It was hard going but with every hour that passed, I felt slightly better. It was during this trek that I noticed that the boots I was wearing were not mine but Marigay's. I smiled and thought that I didn't make it to the top but at least my boots would!

The camp was just below three thousand metres, and once I got there, I slept for four hours straight. The shepherds had transferred our belongings earlier and prepared the tents, so by the time we went down the tents were already made up, and we both slept. By the time the others came, later that afternoon, I woke up, and I was fine. I was hungry for the first time in days, I went to the meals tent and had coffee and toast, and everything stayed down, no more sickness! It was amazing that once I was at an altitude below three thousand metres, I felt fine. After that,

I got steadily better, but I was so exhausted. My trousers were so big on me, they were falling down, so I used the ties on the front of my rucksack to keep my trousers up! Gabriella was taken down to Arusha ahead of us and Susan Harrison almost had a breakdown and left us from the third day. During our climbing it was Becky's birthday, and the cook prepared the tastiest cake apparently; it looked delicious, but since I couldn't eat anything, the cook prepared another one on the last day we were on the mountain to celebrate my recovery and I must say it was the best cake I ever tasted! The organisation of the whole expedition was superb. We saw these trained shepherds, young and old, carrying all the cooking equipment, our tents and belongings, running up and up the steep lanes, and we were just amazed!

Only five members of the group made it all the way to the top, the Uhuru Peak: Maria, Becky, Marianna, Christina and the doctor, accompanied by the shepherds. They all said that although they were exhausted by that time, they didn't appreciate how much harder it would be coming down! The trek wasn't smooth, and they were constantly sliding, which made it extremely difficult. By the time they reached Kibo camp they were close to collapse. They were only allowed to sleep for forty-five minutes and then they had to walk down to the next camp. By the time they arrived they were totally exhausted, but all of them had the magnificent memories of the views from the top to keep them going!

All of us were looking forward to the first shower in the hotel in Arusha. The hotel was described as a four-star facility. However, it was more like a one-star hotel, but by that point, we didn't care! There was a shower and clean sheets, and that was all we needed. One of the other difficulties of this adventure was that all we had to clean ourselves with were the wipes which were used for our hygiene in the tents, cleaning our face and hands and going to the toilet or going al fresco. When we were very high up, we could hear animal voices and after seeing some bright eyes staring at us outside our tent, Marigay and I retreated into our tent, frozen! Our tent was usually next to Deirdre's and Pauline's, and they also had music, perfume and candles so there was always a lovely aura coming over. We could hear each other's conversations, so we teased each other until we fell asleep. Marigay and I negotiated over who would start getting ready for bed first, so one started the bath routine while the other one was getting ready for the next day's requirements. Marigay brought a few body sprays which were very handy to keep us smelling good. All in all, we laughed so much and had such a good time together.

We arrived in Arusha late on a Sunday afternoon and once we were reconnected with the belongings we left behind, then we rushed to our rooms to have our first and long-awaited shower! It was just heaven! A happy, loud dinner followed when we could have alcoholic drinks for the first time. We had lots of laughter and fun! It was a long night with some of the girls joining a few shepherds and going clubbing in the centre of the town on motorcycles! The following day, we went to Zanzibar for a week. We stayed at the Baraza Resort, a palatial, six-star hotel with a beautiful spa and all the luxuries we could have wanted. It was just unbelievable after what we had been through. I said, 'Well, after all the problems I had, I lost weight, and at least I now look great in my bikini!' Overall, it was a great adventure, for a great cause.

After all the money was collected, the CEO, Baroness Delyth Morgan, and the BCN team arranged for all the members of the group who could make it to London to accompany us to visit the BCN Scientific Centre, then to join Baroness Morgan to go to the House of Lords in celebration for our hard work and our achievement in raising so much money for the charity. Some of the ladies came from Cyprus and most of us based in London joined in and we had a wonderful time. We went to the House of Lords for afternoon tea, and to have some drinks in a wine bar nearby.

Meanwhile, I continue to be involved in Breast Cancer Now. The charity puts on two events a year, including the Annual Pink Ribbon Ball. I always go to the ball and sponsor a table, and now they have asked me to be on the committee. I was not sure at first, but I thought about it, spoke to Maria and Philip, and decided that the time commitment was not too much, and I was already doing a lot of the things that they expected the committee members to do. I always made sure that we sponsored at least one table and contributed gifts for the auctions, so why not get closer to a charity I'd always wanted to be involved with? Since I joined the committee, I have met some lovely women, and although I cannot attend all the committee meetings, I keep very close to the group. In fact, I managed to secure four tables in 2019!

Postcards from Antarctica

On 8th November 2016, Mike Bloomberg organised an election party at the Bloomberg Foundation offices in New York. At the time, everyone was convinced that Hillary Clinton would win. I was there with my colleagues from Geller and Bloomberg, and as we were drinking, before the bad news started coming in, we were talking about adventures. I had recently read something about Antarctica in a magazine just before I went to New York, and that must have inspired me, but I remember talking about Antarctica. It seemed natural for me to want to go there, and it was always in the back of my mind, thinking of how I loved visiting Ushuaia and El Calafate in Southern Patagonia in Argentina with my daughter Maria. We stayed in a fabulous hotel inside the Los Glaciares National Park and actually walked on the massive Perito Moreno Glacier. During that trip, we took a boat trip from Ushuaia hoping to see penguins. I loved penguins very much especially after watching the film *Happy Feet*! We were not successful that day, but I always wanted to go back there! I told my colleagues Diane Gubelli and Patti Roskill that I was thinking of going to Antarctica. I said to them, 'Would you be interested in joining me in an Antarctica trip?' and both said, 'Yes, for sure!'

Patti said, 'I was reading something recently about the National Geographic. They do some really amazing expeditions to Antarctica.'

I said, 'OK, leave it with me, and I will check it out and get back to you.'

I went back to the office and called Josh Geller (son of Martin Geller), whose company, Elite Travel, specialise in bespoke adventures. I thought I would just contact Josh to see if he was aware of the National Geographic trips, and he said yes and told me he would get back to me with a few options.

We agreed it would be in early January 2018 because of the timings of everybody's work, which was just fine for me because that was when I was coming back from Cyprus, and I had been planning to go to New York in early January. This time I would meet the girls in New York and go to Antarctica with them. Josh came back to me with a few options, including National Geographic. Another option, which was also very high-end, was the American firm Abercrombie and Kent, who do amazing excursions. Looking at the different options, we still felt a pull towards National Geographic, although Abercrombie and Kent also had options for the Falklands, South Georgia, Easter Island and quite a few other interesting places, for two or three weeks. Again, because of our time constraints and the fact that most of the women who were interested in the trip were businesswomen, we did not have much more time than that, so we thought two weeks, plus a few days in Buenos Aires, would be the maximum we could do. The other reason why we chose National Geographic is that some of the other options came with bigger boats, and bigger boats mean that you don't have landings. For me, the whole point of going to such a remote place was to land so you could be close to the penguins and see all the interesting wildlife in that part of the world in their natural habitat.

After a lot of consultation, we realised we had to act quickly. The discussion started in November, and by the end of December 2016, Josh was telling me, 'If you want to go in January 2018, you have to book as soon as possible, because there are not a lot of cabins left. You need to decide who is coming, how many people, and move very quickly.' I had already met some amazing women in Kilimanjaro, including Deirdre Quinn and her sister Pauline, both friends of Marigay's based in the US. Marigay, of course, was included in our original communications, but there was a conflict with her and Bill because they were going to Rwanda in Africa that same week. As it happened, it turned out that they were going away on a different week, but it was too late by the time she realised that.

There was a lot of pressure for us to decide when we were going, and who was coming with us. My daughter Maria was not able to come; ordinarily she was always part of the team, and in fact this was the first time I had gone anywhere without Maria. Because of the substantial cost, not many people were willing to join us. The group was as follows – Deirdre and her sister Pauline, me, Patti, Diane and Loretta Ucelli, who is a friend of Diane's. I provided information to all the girls with Josh answering all our questions. It came to the crux and we were told that we must book by the next day, commit, pay a deposit and be done with it, otherwise they could give us no guarantees that we would be able to go. We couldn't find twin beds in the cabins (we were going to share) for everyone, because in fact they only had a few cabins on board for one person, so most of them were sharing cabins. Deirdre and Pauline had no problem with sharing a double bed, and we only had one cabin with twin beds, so Diane and Loretta chose that – Diane initially wanted her own room, but we couldn't get one – so we were left with another double-bed cabin, and Patti and I shared that one. I asked if she minded sharing the bed, and she said no, so we said, 'OK, let's do it!' We went for it, put a deposit down and managed to get the last cabins on the ship. We were ecstatic!

As with all these amazing trips, the time beforehand went so quickly, and before we knew it, it was time to make the full payment and finalise the flights. The plan was that we would all fly from New York to Buenos Aires and stay there for the weekend, and then on Monday evening the rest of the participants who could not make it earlier would meet us in Buenos Aires in the hotel for dinner. The following day we would fly by charter flight to Ushuaia, and board the ship from there to Antarctica. Everything was done, and everything we needed was ticked off the lists. National Geographic provided the boots which we rented on arrival at the ship and gave us jackets, and all the gear we needed. We could not go on land with any other shoes apart from those boots, and every time we went in and out, they would have to be decontaminated.

The time had come, and we flew from New York. I was on the same flight as Deirdre; her sister was based in Georgia, so she flew from Atlanta to Buenos Aires, met us at the terminal and the three of us took a taxi into town. The other girls were already there, and we had a fantastic time in Buenos Aires. For some of them it was the first time, but I had obviously been there many times, so I organised some treats for us: tango-dancing shows, dinners, excursions and day trips. We had a tour guide to take us around. The weather could have been better, but despite that, we had some lovely moments, and the food and drink in Argentina was delicious as always, particularly the Mendoza wines! During that time, we really bonded together and had a great time; we indulged ourselves, got massages and treated ourselves to our own silk pillow covers – just silly things, but we had so much fun.

We were all very excited on the flight to Ushuaia. We arrived late in the morning and were taken onto a cruise ship to have lunch along the Ushuaia coast and get to know the other passengers while all our luggage was taken to our cabins at the National Geographic ship. We were mingling with the other passengers and wearing penguin hats that we had bought – six women in penguin hats, so as you can imagine we stood out and looked a bit crazy! Everyone could see we were having so much fun and laughing together, so they wanted to be part of our group, and they were asking us, 'Do you work together?', 'How often do you go on these trips?' as if we'd always known each other. We came back to the port and embarked on the ship, and our adventure started!

The *Explorer* is a beautiful vessel, not very big; we were 148 passengers, which we found funny because Deirdre Quinn's company is called 148 Lafayette, so it was good karma that the number of passengers was 148 – it could just have easily been 150 or 145, so it seemed like a great omen to us. All along the corridors, we could see sick bags, and we knew it was going to be rough. One of the things we were worried about was being sick during the Drake Passage, because those are really treacherous waters, so we all had our anti-nausea patches ready. We arrived on the boat and all of us checked our cabins. Deirdre and Pauline were two doors down from us, and Diane and Loretta were on the opposite side. I agreed with Patti which side of the bed she was sleeping on, and which part of the closet we were hanging our clothes in. It was a beautiful cabin, not huge but very comfortable; our luggage could go under the bed, so it was nice and tidy. We had a little balcony and chairs there, not for sitting there all the time, but when the sun was out it was nice to sit there, covered up, obviously – the bathroom and shower were comfortable and easy to use. We couldn't wait to go for the first dinner. We had also bought a tablecloth from Buenos Aires, so we had our own colourful embroidered cloth on our table. We had all agreed in advance that we would be very polite to the waiters so that they would take care of us and bring us all the wine we wanted. As it happened, there was so much wine we couldn't really finish it!

We had breakfast and dinner in fixed parts of the ship, but for lunch it was more flexible, so we opted to go up to the library, because the library had beautiful wide windows and you could see the incredible views. Breakfast and dinner were in the lower part of the ship; you still had the windows but not the huge space that you had up on top. Every day, we had the wake-up call: 'Good morning, good morning, good morning! Day one...' and the head cabin manager would update us on where we were. We made a lot of progress the first couple of days, but for those days we could still see land, because it took us two days to leave the land behind and enter the Drake Passage. On the first two days, there were no landings, so a lot of presentations and social gatherings took place. We had the speakers, the specialists and the open bar – after dinner there was always something going on up there: documentaries, movies and we could order drinks. We used to go to the gym every day, and we had to book early for massages, because there was a lot of demand. We bought lovely T-shirts with penguins, and again we were told to go to the shop early because they had limited stock and otherwise, we might not have been able to find them in our size. The second night after dinner, we went up to the social room; there was a piano and Patti tried to play. Then we got one of the waiters, who told us he knew how to play the piano, and he did, but not the songs we knew, and we laughed and danced and sang and drank. The following morning, everybody was asking, 'Who was up there last night?' and the answer was always, 'The six girls.' Everybody knew us as the six girls. The food was excellent, five-star hotel quality. The head of entertainment, food and drink was a Swedish guy – he was such an outgoing, fun person, and we spent so much time together. We had different guides circulating with the guests on different tables during dinner, so we had a really good time and learned a lot!

When we arrived in Antarctica, it was so exciting when we started to see the icebergs, initially pieces of ice floating and then getting bigger. On the first landing we saw the penguins and were overwhelmed by the smell, the noise and the colour – their poo is red, and you don't want to be near them when they poo because you'll be in trouble! We stopped at so many beautiful places, like the British Research Centre near the American Research Centre which was active in the 1940s and '50s, and we went to an island where they had the only post office in Antarctica, so we all got postcards and mailed them from there. Maria called me a couple of months after I mailed them and said, 'Guess what just arrived?' And I said, 'I know, mine just arrived too!' The postcards came months later – they arrived in March and we posted them in January.

People from the expeditions also came on board and talked about their experiences. One of the ladies from the UK expedition told us how happy she was to be able to have a shower – it was the first time in a while that they would have been able to have a shower and experience running water and electricity, because they'd stayed in tents for three months with nothing like that, so it was really tough. They gave some amazing speeches. Some of the crew members and scientists also gave presentations, including beautiful photographs of under-sea diving. After the day's events, they would always present to us what we had seen that day, then they told us what would be happening the following day.

In Antarctica, the weather is very unpredictable, but we were lucky when we were there because the weather was so good that we managed to go down further south to Margarita Bay, where the crew and the captain had not actually managed to go for ten years, so it was just as exciting for them as it was for us as many of them had never experienced it either! Our captain Sven, who was Swedish, was also excited and took things as they developed, so sometimes he did not know what we would be doing the following day either. It depended on what the weather was like, but whatever it was, we knew it would be something amazing.

And it was. We saw the killer whales, and the humpbacks – huge whales! Whenever an animal was visible from the ship, we were told to go to the side where you could see it and instructed to look towards two o'clock, or five o'clock or wherever it was. We also saw an albatross, beautiful birds, with wingspans many metres in length. When we got dressed to go outside on a landing, it was a major undertaking because we had to prepare ourselves. We put on three layers of leggings, and then our trousers with the flannel inside and the waterproof trousers, a couple of T-shirts, a jacket and then, over all that, the orange jacket that National Geographic gave everybody, so we all looked the same. Then it was the same with the boots; we had two or three layers of socks and we had to change in the MAD room, where we left our smelly boots and our orange jackets, and our ski poles. We had to wear two or three pairs of gloves because it was so cold, plus hats and sunglasses. All six of us wanted to go out on the same boat, so those of us who got ready faster would be shouting at the others, 'Come on, we're ready to go!'

Patti and I were always shooting ahead, because Patti is exactly like me in that way. And of course, we could not drink too much water because we could not go to the bathroom, so every time before we left the MAD room, we would have to fit in another last-minute toilet visit. If you had to go to the bathroom you had to return to the boat and be decontaminated to remove the bacteria and germs that we all have.

We were there for ten nights. There were many elderly people with grandchildren, and couples celebrating a special occasion, a special birthday or anniversary, but for us it was just because this was something we wanted to do. On the last night going back through the Drake Passage, they told us it was time to put the anti-nausea patch on. In fact, I had put mine on a day earlier and I left it until we came back, because it was quite rough! We arrived in Ushuaia in the afternoon, had dinner and then we were allowed to go outside. It was funny stepping on land for the first time, because we had become so used to walking on the boat. All of us went out for a couple of hours; we did not want to eat or drink anything, just to walk around the small town and get some fresh air. There was another big ship opposite ours on the other side of the port, but it was humongous compared to the size of our ship.

The following morning after breakfast, we had a few hours to tour around Ushuaia, and then we went to the airport and flew back to Buenos Aires. The girls who lived in New York flew straight from Buenos Aires to New York because their flight was much later in the evening. The BA flight that I was on took off at 2:15 in the afternoon, so I missed it. Therefore, I stayed at a hotel near the airport, had dinner at the hotel restaurant – a nice steak and red wine, for the last time – and then the following morning I got up, went to the gym, went to the airport and then came back to London the following Monday morning.

For weeks afterwards, all of us were totally disoriented. We thought that we were still on the ship, and we felt very much like it was moving, even though we were on land. We were told that it is quite common to have that feeling, but I was still surprised to sometimes wake up thinking, 'Where am I? I thought it was Patti next to me!' It is quite amazing how much it affects you. We took a lot of photographs; Diane prepared an album of beautiful pictures, Patti sent the hundreds of photos she took and now we are getting ready for our next adventure.

Exotic Travels

Following the fabulous trip to Antarctica in January 2018, I still had a bucket list: a proper African safari, Bhutan, the Northern Lights in the Arctic, Laos and Cambodia, Iceland, Myanmar, a trip into space, and more. As mentioned earlier, I loved travelling with the family, or with friends and colleagues. Over the years, we have had many adventures in Latin America. I fell in love with Latin America when I first went to Brazil for Bloomberg in 1996. That was the second time I had been to that part of the world because I had accompanied Philip to a medical conference in Rio in 1989. After Rio, we went to Florianópolis, at the most southern part of Brazil, close to Argentina, and stayed with the brother of one of Philip's colleagues who was working with him in London. The family welcomed us even though they didn't speak any English. Their teenage daughter Gabriella spoke limited English and we communicated through her or via the English-to-Portuguese dictionary. I loved Brazil, and as I left, I told myself that I was definitely coming back. I went on a business trip in 1996, and then in 1997, HSBC bought Bamerindus, the local bank in Brazil. After that, they bought banks all over Latin America, and so I had to go to Latin America because of Bloomberg and HSBC. Every year I would go to New York in February and see all my clients, and then Latin America afterwards. The timing was perfect because by then it was summer.

Whenever I was going for business, Maria and I liaised with Journey Latin America. They are one of the best travel agencies because they know Latin America inside out. They organised our itinerary based on our preferences and over the years we visited all of Latin America, apart from Venezuela due to the bad political situation. Nicolas joined us on a few of these trips early on, to Chile and then to Brazil when we visited Rio and the Amazon, and a few years ago, he was the best man to his close friend Sanjeev Lakhani from Haberdashers School, who married a Colombian girl, and the wedding took place in Cartagena, a beautiful city in Colombia. We were all invited, so I met Maria, Nicolas and his fiancée Maria in Cartagena after my business trip and we had a great time at the wedding. After the wedding we went to Guatemala and Belize for an unforgettable holiday! I recall that when we crossed the border from Guatemala to Belize, we were taken by coach to get our passports stamped. We were waiting to get on a little plane to get us to our beach resort in Belize, when we saw a beautiful fish restaurant on the water painted blue and white. We ate some amazing fish and chips, and it felt as if we were back in the UK in Torquay or one of the little English seaside towns, except with lovelier beaches!

The list of places we've visited over the years includes Bolivia (visited La Paz, the capital, and Potosí, a silver mine city where we took a tour of an active silver mine), Ecuador and the Galapagos Islands, Colombia (Bogotá, Cartagena, a coffee plantation farm, an eco-lodge in the jungle), Chile (Santiago, the wine district, and we even visited the breathtaking San Pedro de Atacama in northern Chile), Argentina (Buenos Aires, Mendoza, Ushuaia and El Calafate), Brazil (we made over ten visits, and in one of them, we went to Iguazu Falls with Philip after a business trip to Curitiba where HSBC were headquartered in Brazil), Mexico where Maria joined me (we visited all the sites where Frida Kahlo, the famous painter, lived in Mexico City), Peru and the beautiful city of Cuzco, and of course Machu Picchu! Uruguay and Paraguay are also on the list.

During my trips, all these years, I always felt like I was coming home when I checked in with British Airways. When I arrived at the British Airways counter in Mexico City or wherever I was coming back from, it felt like home because in Latin America you are always at the mercy of the local airlines, and many of them are not great, but the only way to travel is by air.

I feel so blessed because every single adventure I have done, in terms of travel, has been with my children – either Nicolas and Maria, or just Maria. One of the only exceptions was my recent trip to Antarctica – Maria had plans before we finalised the date, so she couldn't make it. It wasn't the same without her; I kept thinking how much she would have enjoyed this and that excursion! Philip had his own work and travelling commitments so he couldn't join me on most of these excursions.

Over the years, I have travelled to South Africa many times on holiday with the family, and primarily on business on my own. Although we went to small local animal reserves, we had never gone to a proper safari adventure. I mentioned this to a couple of my New York colleagues who I knew were very keen on such trips to Africa, to see if they would be interested in joining me.

After a long deliberation as to where to go and what combination of countries to visit that would still be exciting for someone who had visited Africa for safari multiple times, we concluded that south-east Africa would be perfect. That would cover Kenya, Rwanda and Tanzania. Diane Chesnut and I agreed the dates, 1st–13th August 2019. Diane was a colleague at Geller and a dear friend for many years (she came all the way to Cyprus to attend Nicolas and Maria's wedding in September 2014). Diane Gubelli and Loretta Ucelli, who were part of the group that travelled to Antarctica, were also interested in joining us, but when they realised that we planned to visit the gorillas in Rwanda they admitted that they couldn't handle the altitude, so in the end it was just me and Diane. Josh Geller helped us with the itinerary, as he had done with Antarctica. The itinerary was: Nairobi National Park, Maasai Mara Reserve, Volcanoes National Park, Kigali, Northern Serengeti and the Ngorongoro Crater. We flew to Nairobi in Kenya and stayed two nights at the lovely Emakoko Lodge inside Kenya's national park. I understand that this is the only such park located in a big city like Nairobi.

During our stay in Nairobi, we had our first safari outing in the National Park, where we saw plenty of animals but not the 'big five'. We visited David Sheldrick's elephant orphanage, the most successful orphan-elephant rescue and rehabilitation programme in the world, where we saw young and older elephants being fed; the giraffe centre, where huge giraffes came close to us and ate food from our hands; and most importantly, the location where my favourite film *Out of Africa* with Robert Redford and Meryl Streep was filmed. We had a tour of the house where Karen Blixen lived. It was an amazing experience for me because I loved that film so much!

Our next stop was Maasai Mara Reserve, at Cottar's 1920s Safari Camp, a spectacular camp that was rustic but chic. The Maasai Mara, together with Tanzania's Serengeti, form Africa's most famous wildlife park. The image of acacia trees on an endless grass plain epitomises Africa for many, and then add a Maasai warrior and some cattle to the picture and there is no need to add anything further! Upon arrival, our guide took us for a game drive en route to the camp which was spectacular. It was so exciting for me to see all the huge animals right in front of our open Range Rover truck. Everywhere you looked there were beautiful animals: zebras, gazelles, impalas, monkeys, baboons, antelopes, elephants, African buffalo, wallabies; the list goes on and on. We were treated to early morning excursions to see the sunrise and have breakfast in the bush while watching the deep red skies welcoming the sun and the new day. This sight is only experienced in Africa. You can recognise the African scenery as easily as you would recognise a photo of the Maldives or a Greek island! We also had on-foot excursions in the afternoon so we could sit around the fire and watch the romantic sunset while sipping a glass of wine and eating freshly cooked food. On these walks we were joined by our guides and security guards with guns to protect us in case any animals decided to stop by. During our three-day stay, we saw most of the 'big five' African animals: lions, buffalo, rhinos, elephants and leopards. We also saw hyenas, cheetahs, jackals, swine and, of course, vultures.

Arriving in Kigali, we immediately felt that we were on a higher altitude. The air was clean and there was a lot of green vegetation. We drove two and a half hours to Sabyinyo Silverback Lodge, where we stayed one night. In retrospect, we wished we had stayed longer at this lovely lodge because there was a lot more to do in that area than see the mountain gorillas! The following morning, bright and early, we were taken to the Volcanoes National Park, best known as a sanctuary for the region's rare mountain gorillas. There are eight families of mountain gorillas living on the slopes of the Virunga Mountains. Visitors were put into small groups and prior to departure we were given a briefing by park staff, assigned a gorilla family to visit and rangers to guide us. The guides usually go up the mountain the night before, so they know where each gorilla family is to make it easier for the tourists. The treks take place in the slopes of the Virunga Volcanoes, so you need to be in good physical condition. We had to go through thick vegetation, up and up, with our guides having to cut back the plants so we could pass. We were lucky that after four hours, we saw our first gorilla. The animals are used to seeing people, so they continue with their routine and don't pay too much attention to their visitors. We saw a whole family, from the huge male silverback to the mother and siblings of various ages. They behaved like a human family with the same habits and characteristics: yawning, scratching and lying back on their hands. We could go very near them for photos, which was exciting! The maximum time we could spend with them was an hour, and it flew by very fast. Before long, we were on our way down the mountain, heading towards our lodge. After an enjoyable lunch there, our guide drove us back to Kigali towards our five-star hotel, the Kigali Serena Hotel.

During our drive back to the city, our driver suggested that if we arrived early enough, we could visit the Kigali Genocide Memorial, which was very much worth seeing. Thankfully, we made it on time, and we were allowed in. What we saw and heard from the photos, videos and recordings was indeed very emotional! In just a hundred days in 1994, about eight hundred thousand people were slaughtered in Rwanda by ethnic Hutu extremists. They were targeting members of the minority Tutsi community, as well as their political opponents, irrespective of their ethnic origin. The French were accused of supporting the Hutus and not doing enough to stop the killings. The UN, who were desperately trying to get more help from overseas, were unsuccessful but managed to shelter some people in the UN buildings before they had to evacuate. What really impressed us, however, was the fact that the people have moved on, and although they will never forget what happened, they now live in harmony with each other, which is incredible.

Our evening at the Serena Hotel was very enjoyable because we had all the luxuries that we were used to including hairdryers! The following morning, we flew from Kigali International Airport to Serengeti North in Tanzania and to Alex Walker's Serian Serengeti North Camp, a traditional safari tent. This camp is open from June to November to take advantage of the huge herds of wildebeest in the Great Migration which are frequent in that area during these months. It took us some time to get used to not having running water and having to use a bucket shower and electricity for a certain number of hours. At night, we could hear the animals outside our tent which was exciting and scary at the same time, but after the first night, we got used to it. In fact, our stay in Serengeti was the most memorable because we saw all the big five African animals and were also lucky enough to see multiple crossings of the Mara River of wildebeest, a sight never to be forgotten. Hundreds of animals gathered on one side of the wide river, and we could see the long black lines of animals running over vast plains, segregating at the edge of the river but taking their time before they crossed. Once the first animal ran into the river, then all the rest followed. Interestingly, the first wildebeest followed a few zebras who always made the first move! Unbelievable and unforgettable.

Our last stop was the Ngorongoro Crater. We stayed at the Ngorongoro Crater Lodge, which is recognised as one of the best lodges on the continent. It was by far the most luxurious lodge we could have imagined. However, it was way over the top, with chandeliers and expensive art pieces which we felt were a bit too much. The whole experience was disappointing because due to the timing of our visit (winter in Africa), there were no rains, so the crater was rather brownish without much water and therefore not many animals around. We stayed two nights and we relaxed with bathtubs, champagne and five-star hotel food, so it was not all that bad! By this time, we were eager to return to Nairobi and fly back home. Diane flew back to London with me, so it was good to start and to end the trip together at Heathrow Airport. The great African adventure had come to an end but with lots of memories to last forever, and I still have the rest of my bucket-list destinations to visit!

Iris

2019 was a fabulous year. In late 2018, I decided that I wanted to stop my consulting contract with Wargaming since I believed that I had delivered all that was expected from me as part of my contractual obligations. By then, we had a strong tax department, all the global tax issues had been resolved and we had trained the top leadership as well as the middle management on what they could and could not do when travelling on business to the various countries where Wargaming had offices. My work with the CEO was steady but nothing exciting, and my relationship with the CFO was good. However, I didn't feel that I could add much more, or to put it another way, that there was no willingness to use me to the full potential of what value I could have added!

31st January 2019 was my last day at Wargaming and we planned a small farewell party at a lovely restaurant in the old Nicosia district. By coincidence, Nicolas was on a business trip in Cyprus and Philip was also there since he had stayed after the Christmas holidays. I went to New York on business in mid-January and then flew back to Cyprus for the last week to work at Wargaming. The farewell party was fun, and the CEO gave a lovely speech thanking me for all my contribution during the five years I worked for them. We had a bit too much to drink, but overall, it was both a happy and sad occasion since it was time for closure.

We returned to London after Miranda's fiftieth birthday party on 2nd February, which was a glamorous event at the new Radisson Blu hotel in Larnaca with plenty of yummy food and lots of drinks and music. All our family and friends were there, and we danced until the early hours. When we got back to London, Nicolas and his wife Maria dropped by for coffee and they told us the amazing news that Maria was expecting a baby! We were thrilled with the news, and we started dancing, crying and hugging each other. That was the best news indeed. The baby was due in late September, and we couldn't wait for its arrival!

For my sixty-fifth birthday on 22nd May, we organised a trip to the Amalfi Coast since all of us wanted to visit it and had not managed to do so. In addition, since Maria was by then five months pregnant, we didn't want to travel too far. We had a wonderful time with a full itinerary. We started by vising Portofino, a very picturesque port town with many cruise ships and lovely shops. The whole place was full of beautiful, colourful and aromatic flowers. From there, on our way to Naples, we stopped at the historic town of Genoa with its medieval castles and beautifully preserved old buildings. We flew to Naples and then drove to Positano on narrow and winding roads with the sea deep down below us. We used Positano as our base and from there we visited many small villages, each one with its own charm, as well as the glamorous and iconic Island of Capri. We went there by boat and climbed its steep and winding roads to get to the top. The views from there were spectacular!

While in Positano, Maria's girlfriend Nisrine joined us for the last four days of our trip. By then, they had been seeing each other for over a year so it was a good way to spend some time with her and for Nisrine to also get to know us better. It went extremely well, and we could see that they were very happy together. We had never seen Maria so happy, so we were hoping that Nisrine would be the one – and that's exactly what happened. After our summer holidays in Cyprus, on 7th September Maria and Nisrine announced to us that they were engaged. We returned to London on 13th September and were able to attend a very intimate engagement celebration at Maria's flat in Maida Vale the following day. Nisrine's brother Hadi came from Paris, where he was living, to attend on behalf of Nisrine's family since her parents and sister couldn't make it – they lived in Lebanon. We were so happy to see them together because it was obvious that they were in love!

By then we knew that Nicolas and his wife Maria were expecting a girl and the due date was 26th September, so there was not long to go. We were all very excited and I was hoping that our granddaughter would arrive on time since I was planning to be on a business trip to New York between the 16th and 21st of September. On the same day, 21st September, Maria's mum Nitsa was due to arrive from Cyprus and spend a few months with them to assist them when the baby arrived. They told us that they were planning to call the baby Iris, which represents a beautiful flower. In Greek mythology, Iris was the goddess of good news and the rainbow represented her. All was progressing well and on Thursday 26th September, the due date, Maria started having contractions, so Nicolas took her to the local Barnet Hospital, as planned. We joined them as soon as we were told and after several hours the doctor told us it was best if we left for the night because it looked like the birth wasn't imminent. That must have been around 11pm, so Nitsa came home with us and we were expecting Nicolas's call to tell us the good news. His call arrived after midnight, so Iris was born on 27th September and both baby and mum were doing very well. After a few hours of sleep, we woke up early, excited and eager to go to the hospital and welcome our lovely Iris. We stopped at a florist on the way and bought some beautiful pink roses. Interestingly, on that Friday morning, the sky was alight with a huge and colourful rainbow to welcome our Iris!

We were all very emotional when we saw the tiny bundle of joy in Maria's arms. To us, she looked very beautiful even though we were aware that we were biased! Maria and Iris were doing very well so they were discharged by the end of the day. The days and months passed very quickly, and I carried a lot of photos with me during my regular New York business trips. Everyone had to see the photos of my beautiful granddaughter!

In November, Philip and I flew to Bucharest, the capital of Romania, to celebrate our goddaughter Stefania's thirtieth birthday. Her parents Maro and Andreas came from Cyprus as well as our dear friends Egly, her brother Harris and his friend Kyriakos Ioannou, a lovely young doctor who was working at a prominent private hospital in Nicosia. Stefania's big day was on Sunday 17th November, so we packed as much as we could in our brief visit. We spent the day before Stefania's birthday exploring Bucharest and its lovely sights. The following day, we had an early breakfast and then a driver took us to the Transylvanian region, or as it is commonly known, the Dracula region. It was a wonderful trip and we all very much enjoyed the mountainous views and of course, we loved exploring Dracula's castle! We returned to Bucharest in the early evening, tired but happy with our excursion and excited at the prospect of a fabulous birthday celebration dinner. Harris organised the whole dinner with the appropriate champagne and wines to accompany each dish. We opened all the presents to Stefania's excited cries! A lovely birthday cake ended the amazing dinner celebration. We all flew home – Philip and I to London, Stefania to Athens, where she was living and working, and the rest of the group back to Cyprus. It was a short but very special weekend for all of us.

The Pandemic

2019 was edging to a close and after my last New York business trip of the year, I returned to London on 21st December, excited at the prospect of spending the holidays in London with the family and our gorgeous granddaughter - our first Christmas with Iris! In addition, my goddaughter Stefania, my nephew Xenakis, his wife Miranda and their two lovely daughters, Thekla and Kyriaki, were planning on visiting and spending Christmas and New Year with us. Stefania was coming from Athens while Xenakis and his family were coming from Aradippou. Our *symbethera* Nitsa (my daughter-in-law Maria's mum) was also in London. She had arrived from Cyprus before Iris was born and was due to return to Cyprus on New Year's Day. It was going to be a great Christmas.

And it was! We spent Christmas Day at Nicolas and Maria's house since Iris was just three months old then. During the celebrations we heard on the news about a new virus called COVID-19 that was identified in Wuhan, China, a city of eleven million people. This virus was another strain of the SARS virus, which was a big threat in the 1990s, primarily in Asia. At the time, not enough information was available and the COVID threat seemed very, very far away. If we only knew!

On 26th December, Boxing Day, we hosted lunch at our house, which included my dear friend Marigay and her mother

Pilli. Marigay was visiting the UK from New York, where she lived with her fiancé Bill Ford. Her mother was unwell, so she came to visit her and decided to stay over the holidays. We had a very enjoyable day with all the family and our visitors. Iris was wearing her new red dress and she was the centre of attention as usual. New Year's Eve was spent at a local Italian restaurant for convenience, so the new parents were not too far away from their baby. Overall, we had wonderful holiday celebrations and, one by one, all our guests returned to their homes. 2020 was looking to be a fantastic year! In mid-March, I was to participate in an Arctic adventure with my friends. In early April, we planned to go to Cyprus for Greek Easter and have Iris's christening on 12th April. On 26th May, Maria and Nisrine were getting married at their dream venue, Aynhoe Park in Oxfordshire. What could possibly go wrong?

With the arrival of 2020, our planned expedition to the Arctic in mid-March felt closer than ever. A group of eight, all female, were going to do a snowshoe trek in the Arctic for seven nights. The group was made up of Marigay, Deirdre, Pauline and Martha from the US, and from the UK, me, Linda, Meribeth and Mary. Caroline had a foot injury, so she had to pull out. The plan was to all meet in Stockholm, Sweden, have a couple of nights there and then fly to Kiruna, where we would start our trek. During the day we would walk for six to eight hours and at night we would stay at wooden igloos. The highlight of the trip was the chance of witnessing the majestic dancing skies of the Northern Lights. At the end of the trek, we would stay at the Ice Hotel for one night and at the 'normal' Ice Hotel for the last night. We would then fly from Kiruna to Stockholm and back to London or New York, as appropriate.

When Marigay was in London during the Christmas holidays, she suggested that it would be a good idea to get some training wearing the special snowshoes that we would need for our trek, so she invited all of us to join her at Bill's house in Vail, Colorado, in late January. At that time, there would be plenty of snow so we could practice. As I was in New York in late January for business, I agreed to go. The rest of the team members from London couldn't make it so in the end it was Marigay, myself, Deirdre and her sister Pauline. We all arrived in Vail on 16th January and stayed there until Monday 20th January. Monday was a public holiday in the US (Martin Luther King Jr. Day), so it worked very well. It was the first time I had visited Vail and I was delighted. It is a fabulous town and the scenery with the trees, bushes and snow made everything looking magical! We had a fantastic time. We laughed so much! In addition to the snowshoe-practising, we did some shopping for the trip, had some amazing food in the top restaurants and watched films at night until very late. At the end of the trip, we all felt that we were ready for the adventure!

Life continued and so did my trips to New York in February and early March. During these months, news coverage of the new COVID virus in Asia was increasing with reports indicating that cases of the virus had been found in many countries in Europe and the US. Even at that time, not much was known about the virus and how people could respond to it. The main symptoms were a dry cough, high temperature, loss of smell and pain all over the body. By the time I returned to London from New York on 7th March, things were getting more and more unsettling. Reports of people dying from COVID increased and everyone seemed very worried and concerned. The Arctic group still thought that the trip would go ahead, so Marigay arrived in London on 12th March, two days before we were due to fly to Stockholm. Meanwhile, Deirdre announced that she and Pauline would not join us due to the uncertainty and what was happening to Deirdre's business in China; she couldn't risk being stuck in Europe and unable to return to the US. On Friday 13th March, our British Airways flights to Stockholm were cancelled and so was the trip. Marigay managed to get back to New York before the US imposed restrictions for non-US citizens returning to the US from Europe, including the UK.

Meanwhile, Philip was in Cyprus awaiting my visit there after my North Pole trek. He had stayed in Cyprus when I left for my business trip to New York since I had that trip plus the Arctic trip. The whole family was expected to travel to Cyprus in April for the Greek Orthodox Easter celebrations as well as for Iris's christening. Therefore, since there was no food in the house, on Saturday 14th March I went and did a lot of shopping since people were panicking that there would soon be lockdowns and food shortages. I had to wait in long queues to pay for the shopping and I was very glad to be back home! I invited Nicolas and his family as well as Maria and her fiancée Nisrine to come to our house for lunch the following day, so I could see them before I flew to Cyprus the following week to be with Philip and then return together to London. It was lovely being all together again, although Nicolas wasn't one hundred per cent OK. He had an upset stomach and headache, and he thought it was due to being out late the previous night. After everyone left and while I was clearing things and cleaning up, my friend Marianna called me from Larnaca and told me that the Cyprus president had just made a public announcement that as of 6pm local time on Monday 16th March, anyone arriving in Cyprus from the UK would have to quarantine for fourteen days at one of the government's prescribed hotels. However, if one arrived before 6pm, then they could self-quarantine at their own homes. I immediately called British Airways and managed to get the last seat on the early flight at 7:35am, which arrived in Cyprus at 2pm. I knew that I had to go and be with Philip because I felt that this crisis would last for longer than anyone anticipated. I arrived in Cyprus and had to isolate at home for ten days. And the pandemic was upon us just like that!

When I called the children to inform them that I had arrived safely, Nicolas told me that he wasn't feeling at all well, and by then, he had all the symptoms of COVID: high temperature, constant dry cough, loss of smell, very bad headaches and pain all over his body. There was no help from his GP, and when he called the NHS 111 helpline, as instructed in the media by the government medical advisor, no one picked up. It was ringing and ringing for hours and hours. The only thing that he could do was to take painkillers such as paracetamol, and nothing else. Philip and I were very concerned about Nicolas and his wife Maria and baby Iris.

Nicolas's appetite vanished and he wasn't eating much, so he lost eight kilos in two weeks. When we had FaceTime calls, he looked really unwell and gaunt. He isolated from Maria and Iris as far as possible, and although Maria had very mild symptoms, she didn't feel as bad as Nicolas and Iris also appeared to be fine. We talked to Maria and Nisrine, and they went by Nicolas's house to leave paracetamol and food outside their door. They ran out of painkillers and food. The situation was getting worse by the day, and we didn't know what to do. We were hearing all kinds of horror stories about people who were unwell, that some of them who went into the hospital died and no one could see them or accompany them since the virus was so contagious, so Nicolas and the rest of us concluded that he was better off staying at home. By the second week, when he was getting very weak, we all thought that he should go to the hospital, but thank God, from that day onwards, he started feeling a bit better each day until he fully recovered. It took him months to get over the virus and he still looked so skinny for someone as tall as Nicolas, over six foot four, but we were all relieved that he was better, and that Maria and Iris had been spared.

The UK finally introduced lockdown on 23rd March, much later than other European countries and the rest of the world. On 16th

April, the lockdown was extended for a further three weeks and all people had to stay home and work from home. On 10th May, the Prime Minister announced a conditional plan for lifting lockdown and said that people who couldn't work from home could return to work but to avoid the use of public transport. Wearing masks any time we went out, continually washing our hands and ensuring that the food that was delivered at home was cleaned thoroughly with antiseptic products became the routine and norm. On 1st June, the phased reopening of schools in England started and by 15th June, non-essential jobs in England also reopened. By mid-August, lockdown restrictions eased further, with indoor theatres, bowling alleys and so on also opening.

Meanwhile in Cyprus, from 16th March, people with COVID-free medical certificates could enter the country but they had to quarantine for fourteen days in hotels which were now opened to accommodate quarantining people. The cost was met by the travellers. On 24th March, we were also on lockdown with an E150 fine for each violation. From 30th March, stricter rules applied with curfew from 9pm to 6am and the fine for each violation doubled to E300. The government introduced a very sophisticated system which was strictly monitored. We could only go out once per day after we received an authorisation code from the government's central IT system. If you were caught out without the authorised code, you were fined E300 on the spot. You could only go out for exercise, to the pharmacy or doctor, or to the supermarket. Our routine was that Philip would go out to the supermarket or the pharmacy as needed, and I would go for my daily run or walk. It was really weird that we didn't see anyone coming by our beach house as was the case before, because it was prohibited to even walk by the sea. That included us, who had the beach as our back yard!

This lockdown lasted from March until 21st May. From that day, we could meet with a maximum of ten people, and we could go out with the authorisation codes up to three times per day. The schools also reopened on that day. That was something really big! Since my birthday was on 22nd May, we hosted a small dinner party for some very, very close friends and family. It was the first time we'd had company and seen people since the pandemic began, so we were all delighted! We sat in our veranda under the stars with the waves as background music. On 9th June, the airport reopened, and the first flights arrived from authorised countries where the cases were under control.

Cyprus was excellent for us at that time and we felt safer than being in London. The weather was perfect, sunny and warm every day, and we had the beach that we could use again after 21st May. But we missed our children and Iris terribly – that was the worst thing! – so, we were all praying that things would continue to improve so that they could all visit us. By the end of March, during the lockdowns in the UK and Cyprus, we realised that there was no way we could proceed with the christening or with Maria and Nisrine's wedding, so we postponed both events. We finally booked the wedding for 26th August in the UK and the christening for 10th October in Cyprus since all Maria's family and most of mine were based there.

During spring and early summer, when the coronavirus was rampant throughout Europe, we all watched in horror, on TV and through social media outlets, the suffering and death toll of thousands and thousands of people. Since coronavirus impacted breathing, patients with serious breathing issues needed oxygen and special ventilators to help them breathe and therefore survive. All hospitals across Europe and beyond were overwhelmed with the high number of patients admitted, so doctors had to act like gods – they had to choose which patients to treat on the basis that they had a better chance of surviving than others. Most hospitals ran out of ventilators and doctors/nurses' personal protective equipment (PPE). China, where the virus was first detected, and which was therefore further ahead than the Western world, managed to control the spread of the virus and started sending PPE and other technical equipment to other countries. The UK government was criticised by many commentators and the general population when they heard that the care homes for the elderly had the highest percentage of fatalities due to mistakes, inaction and late measures introduced by the government. We were all glued to our social media outlets for the latest news and updates on the work done on potential vaccines by the pharmaceutical companies and research laboratories globally. Regrettably many conspiracy theories were invented and believed by too many worldwide!

With all the promising news that vaccines could be ready as early as late 2020, people started hoping that perhaps we would pass the worst of this nightmare by the summer of 2021. Indeed, the UK enjoyed the best summer for decades which helped people when they were allowed to go out during and after the lockdown. Had we seen the back of this pandemic? Were mandatory mask-wearing, hand sanitisers and food queues coming to an end? Would life as we knew it and travelling commence again? We all missed our ability to travel freely and hug each other, and attend big events, whether family, social or sports. No one would have thought that this virus would still be around in 2022 and beyond! Over one million people died globally by the summer and the horrifying statistics kept going up and up.

Back to the Village

When the UK went into lockdown, Maria and Nisrine decided that it made more sense to leave their flat in Maida Vale and move into our house in Winchmore Hill in North London so that they had more space to work and also for Zeus, their young dog, to be able to run and explore our garden. With the weather so lovely, it was better for them to have the larger house to live in. Since remote working became mandatory, they each needed an office and a desk to work from. They had Zoom calls constantly all day, so they couldn't share one desk or table. Our house enabled one of them to use the office we had upstairs and the other one to use either Nicolas's old room, which had a desk built in, or the long table in the living room.

We all knew that we didn't plan to return to London any time soon, so we were delighted with their suggestion! This meant that we would have them house-sitting and taking care of it in our long absence. Our plants would be watered, our mail would be reviewed and any urgent requests could be dealt with in a timelier manner. Also, very importantly, they would be closer to Nicolas and his family since our house was only ten minutes away from theirs. The girls settled down very well in their new home, and so did Zeus, who loved to sit at the top of the garden steps and supervise his domain! They stayed there until we returned to London on 22nd August so we could attend their wedding.

During their stay in Winchmore Hill, they started looking to buy a house. They realised that, having Zeus, they needed more space, and although they loved their flat in Maida Vale, they lived on the top floor, the fifth, so after a while it was a big chore having to take him out twice daily for walks. It was also time for them to move somewhere closer to us. Despite the restrictions, they eventually managed to view some houses they really liked, and by late August, they put a deposit on a lovely house in Kensal Green in NW10, which was still in Central London, only ten minutes from Maida Vale and now only thirty minutes from Winchmore Hill. We visited the house when we were back in London.

By August 2020, things were looking better and some of the restrictions were eased so finally Nicolas and his family were able to fly to Cyprus on 1st August, and Maria arrived with Nisrine the following day. We were delighted to see them all. However, we felt very emotional that Iris didn't recognise us at all. She'd only been a baby when we last saw her, and now she was eight months old, very grown up! But it didn't take long for her to get used to us and be comfortable and smiling every time she saw us. During this time, we took advantage of all of us being together to host a small family gathering in a local taverna in Aradippou so everyone in our family would meet Nisrine, since most of them had never met her. It was a really fun evening at the Kazani Taverna. We managed to have a band which played popular music and we even danced! Before long, we all had to return to London and get ready for the wedding.

Maria and Nisrine loved the Aynhoe Park venue in Oxfordshire and were determined to get married there. However, due to the pandemic and the various lockdowns and restrictions imposed on all of us, there had been so many cancellations which led the owner of this beautiful but private venue to decide that he would close it down as of the New Year – no more wedding receptions!

Once Maria and Nisrine heard about this, they decided to proceed with the wedding despite the COVID restrictions. Under the rules at the time, weddings could only proceed on a very small basis with thirty people in total, including the two registrars, the photographer and video people, the DJ, the hotel staff, etc. Taking all of those into account, we could only have a total of twenty people including us. Even baby Iris counted for one person! Since all the preparations were already made and all details agreed from the spring, we only had to inform the various suppliers of the smaller number of guests. We also had the unpleasant task of informing the guests we invited early on that due to the restrictions, we were limited as to the numbers that could attend the wedding. They were of course very understanding. We all faced the same challenges! We had the whole venue at our disposal, and we were very happy that Nisrine's parents Rima and Sami were able to fly over from Beirut, and her brother Hadi was also able to join us from Paris. Nisrine's sister Farah was living in London at the time, so their whole immediate family were present. Unfortunately, none of my family and friends in London or Cyprus could join us. Therefore, we only invited my cousin Elli's daughter Stavroula and her husband Bambos plus Maria's godfather George. The rest of the guests were the girls' closest friends without spouses! The wedding was taking place on Wednesday 26th August, so we all arrived at Aynhoe Park on Tuesday afternoon. That evening we had a barbeque outdoors with lots of drinks and got into the spirit of the event.

Even though it was a small gathering, we had a fabulous time! The photographer Robert Shack and his assistant did a fantastic job and didn't disappoint us. Like the amazing photos and video that he produced for Nicolas's engagement party and wedding, the albums and video of the wedding were spectacular! The venue inside and the grounds outside assisted his capturing of their beauty. We were also very lucky with the weather, and we even had sunshine during the champagne reception after the wedding ceremony. We were all very emotional when each girl walked into the wedding chapel on the arm of their respective fathers. We followed all the Cypriot customs and so did Rima and Sami with the Lebanese customs. The dinner was excellent, and after the amazing food and plenty of drinks, the speeches provided a lot of emotion and laughter. We then enjoyed beautiful music in Greek, Arabic and English. We danced for a very long time into the night. All the young guests then retreated to the special cove basement for more music, snacks and drinks. Iris behaved impeccably and enjoyed with curiosity what was going on around us. Maria and Nicolas hired a babysitter who took care of Iris when she was ready to sleep. The following morning, after a sumptuous breakfast, our guests left. The immediate family stayed on for lunch and after a lot of exciting discussions and photos, we all felt that the wedding was a huge success, and it was time to return home. Maria and Nisrine left early in the morning for their mini honeymoon at Costa Navarino, near Kalamata in Greece. Their 'proper' honeymoon was rescheduled for December in the Maldives. They had a fabulous time on both honeymoons.

After the wedding, our attention turned to organising Iris's christening in Cyprus. Everyone was saying to us that we should have had the christening done during August when we were all in Cyprus because no one knew how the COVID situation would be by the autumn. However, we stuck to our guns and planned for 10th October, hoping for the best. The situation in the UK, Cyprus and elsewhere was constantly changing. In Cyprus, people were allowed to have weddings, christenings and so on for a maximum of a hundred people in October, so we felt OK to proceed. Although we invited a hundred guests, some of them still felt unsafe to attend an indoor event so they declined. In the end we had eighty-five guests, which was a very good number.

The christening took place at St Nikolaos Church in Dhekelia, a beautiful little church on the shores of the sea in Larnaca. It was less than ten minutes from our house. I talked to the priest and we were all set to be there for twelve noon and then to go to Galu, a beautiful seaside venue, also in Larnaca and five minutes from our house, at 1pm. Maria organised everything from the UK and finished the details once she arrived in Cyprus. We flew together with Maria and Iris on 30th September so we could take care of the last bits and pieces while Nicolas arrived a few days later. The godparents were Maria, my daughter and Iris's aunt, as well as Evi, Maria C's sister and also Iris's aunt. Maria and Nicolas decided that it was better to ask each of their only siblings to be the godmother or *nona* in Greek. This would ensure that both would be in Iris's life for the long term.

The day arrived and it was a beautiful sunny and hot day for October. We all got ready, and Maria, Nicolas and Iris, who were staying in Nicosia with Maria's parents, passed by our house so we all left together for the church. We arrived there at noon and soon after everyone was there. The ceremony was very enjoyable, although Iris, like all babies being christened, eventually started crying. Initially she was very calm and smiling to everyone even when Evi and Maria were holding her. She was curious to observe the priest with his imposing black clothing and big golden cross across his chest. However, when she was totally undressed and the priest started putting her into the water basin chanting the psalms, she started crying very hard. She wanted her mum, but Maria wasn't allowed to touch her until after the ceremony ended and the *nones* handed the baby back to her, so she had to endure Iris's crying like all of us. It didn't last too long. Once the baptism finished, the priest handed Iris to the *nones* so they could dress the baby with the new clothes and cross. They then held her while the priest concluded the final part of the ceremony, and finally, they handed Iris to her mother. By then, Iris was fine and no longer crying, but she was very happy to be in her mother's arms again. Lots of photos were taken by the photographer before, during and after the ceremony. Once all that was done, we left the church and headed for Galu and the delicious lunch that was awaiting. Usually by that time, the christened baby would be too tired after the 'ordeal' they had gone through and would fall asleep, but not Iris! She stayed awake throughout the party that followed and didn't sleep until we went to our house late in the afternoon.

Galu was beautifully decorated in pink, white and light gold balloons, with a huge colourful rainbow as the backdrop, fittingly as Iris's name is taken from the Greek goddess Iris, the goddess of good news and rainbows. The tables were set in similar colours and the whole room looked spectacular. The food was delicious and the drinks plentiful. By 6pm everyone departed, and the immediate family gathered at our house to relax. We were all very happy that Iris was finally christened, and all our big gatherings were finished, with no more worries about the latest COVID announcements as to how many people were allowed to congregate, and so on.

After a relaxing week or so, the family returned to the UK while Philip and I stayed until 9th November. By that time, the UK Prime Minister Boris Johnson imposed a second national lockdown in England. The guidelines kept changing and the UK government eventually imposed Tier 4 restrictions in London and south-east England from 21st December. So, for the 2020 Christmas, we gathered at Maria and Nisrine's new house with Nicolas and his family. Nisrine's brother Hadi joined us from Paris, and her sister Farah was in London, so she also attended. It was a low-key event even though we were all so happy to be together again after the recent lockdown we'd had to go through. Everyone was wondering when this nightmare would end!

In mid-December 2020, the first vaccinations against COVID-19 took place in the US and UK, and it was with this hopeful news that we could look forward to 2021 as a family. News of the vaccine meant that we could start thinking about the world opening again, and what it would be like when we could travel properly and see some of the people that we might not have seen all year. However, we knew things would not go back to normal immediately, and perhaps not for quite some time.

Epilogue: More than a Dream

Looking back, I feel as though my life has been more than a dream, because I never thought I would have the life I had. It exceeded all my wildest expectations of what life would bring for me when I was growing up in a small village in Cyprus. I never imagined a life like this, since in those days I did not even expect to be allowed to go to England to study and go to university. As a result of my surroundings, my thinking and my horizons were much more limited.

I think I've been very lucky to have such a successful career and a beautiful, fantastic family, and that means everything to me. I have met so many incredible people, both from the corporate world and among my clients, as well as colleagues and other friends along the way. I continue to meet people and become friends with them, which is still a great source of pleasure.

The US offered me a career in tax, an area that I initially knew nothing about. When we returned to London, I got into the accounting world, with tax, albeit initially a different type – and the rest is history! Also, I never had to take time off because I'd already had my children, unlike some of my colleagues and peers, who had to take career breaks. I was thirty-two when I came back from America, and I was twenty-six and twenty-eight when my children were born, so with the help of Philip and my in-laws, I could focus on progressing my career.

While my knowledge and experience has grown over the years, I still hold on to the same values I had as a young village girl. I think the number-one value for me is the appreciation of what one has. When I was growing up, we were well off and we had a very comfortable middle-class lifestyle, but everyone was expected to chip in and work. Since my dad was an entrepreneur, there were many opportunities for us to actually work, and that has really set me on the course of being hard-working, respectful and dealing with customers from a young age, particularly the women in my village. All that helped me in later life, not in Houston so much but when I got into the real world of business and having clients and keeping the level of service they expected, that was at the very core of who I became as an adult. This was all quite unlike my mother, whose life focused on the children and being at home. My sisters were different from me; I was the youngest daughter, and I was the only one interested in the business, even my brothers were not very keen, so that in a way shaped my life and my love for work. Even now, if I had to choose between cooking and running or working, I choose running and work. I cook because I have to, and when I'm entertaining, but it does not have that natural appeal to me.

Having a stable marriage for over four decades was also a very stabilising factor in my busy life! What makes a successful marriage? We celebrated our forty-first anniversary for our church wedding on Monday 11th June 2019. Philip and I have two anniversaries – the first one on 19th November 1977, which is when we had our civil wedding in London, and then the church wedding on 11th June 1978 in Aradippou. I think that, for a strong, long-lasting marriage, you have to compromise; you have to give and take. You must not be selfish. You must realise that the feelings and the relationship change and evolve over the years. You have to respect and support each other; all these elements make a great marriage. And I'm not saying it in a bad way, but the fact that I travelled a lot helped keep the passion and the loving fresh, because you miss each other! I think that worked very well for us. You looked forward to coming home. The problems start when you don't look forward to coming home! That's when something is wrong. I'm always excited about leaving and travelling; I know I have itchy feet. But when I turn into Eversley Crescent, it's the best place to be. It could be raining, snowing: I don't care; I'm home. That, to me, is very important.

The pandemic disrupted my business routine and the monthly trips to New York. In fact, 3rd–6th March 2020 was the last trip, and I visited again in mid-November 2021, which seemed like a decade had passed and not only eighteen months. The world of global business trips has changed fundamentally, so going forward, I expect to visit New York for business maximum twice per year. With the international tourist industry opening up again, it is time to revisit my bucket list.

I was delighted that finally, in March 2022, myself and five friends (Marigay, Meribeth, Mary, Deirdre and Pauline) completed our Arctic adventure which was postponed from March 2020 due to the pandemic.

Furthermore, the arrival of our first grandchild, Iris, on 27th September 2019, has changed our life! Since then, I missed her very much when I was away on my monthly business trips to New York. During the pandemic, we were apart for over six months in 2020, but in 2021, we ensured that we were not overseas for too long. We did not want to miss out on her growing up, so we planned our lives in a way that meant we were in Cyprus at the same time for at least some of the time.

Of course, from the perspective of family, we look forward to having more grandchildren. When our daughter Maria got married, this became a real possibility. In fact, on 15th July 2022, our handsome Raphael was born! He weighed 3.5 kilos and is a very tall baby! Maria had a good pregnancy, and both she and the baby recovered well. I stayed with Maria, Nisrine and the baby for a week to help them settle into a routine and I now spend weekends with them as they adjust to their new lifestyle. Their dog Zeus is also adjusting to having a baby in the house and to share his parents' love and attention. He is a good dog, friendly and very gentle. Iris adores her little cousin and is so excited every time she visits Raphael, wanting to mother him, hold him, feed him and even change him! Nicolas and his wife Maria are also planning to have more children in due course, so both Philip and I will help them as much as we can.

Overall, apart from the hiccups with my illness, and later, Philip's problems because of 7/7, I know I have a lot to be grateful for. My work has been amazing, I never really encountered any serious prejudice and I did not compete with any men because there were no men on an equal footing with me whom I might have competed with! Looking back, I have had a blessed life and no regrets at all. I have never expected to reach the professional level I have reached, so I am thankful for that. I'm very comfortable with my age. What scares me is death. Nobody wants to die, but when you have a full cycle of life – and I saw this with my dad – you might be ready to go. I don't know how things will be in twenty years' time, but obviously if you are in good health and you have a good quality of life you don't want to die. I know people in their nineties who are driving, living on their own, cooking and taking care of themselves. I hope, God willing, I will be one of them, because so far it has been a great life and an amazing journey.

I would be extremely fulfilled if I succeeded in my dream to go into space. That's something I am still very much working towards, and I hope that within the next decade, while I am still functional, I can make the journey into space, whatever that means. I think there is definitely an enthusiasm and an expectation that things will happen very quickly, and now there are more people getting involved who have had great success in other industries such as computing. At first, it was mainly Richard Branson, but now Jeff Bezos and Elon Musk are involved, things seem to have speeded up. NASA, in their US programme, are looking to go to Mars, so who knows what will happen in the future. It fascinates me still; it's something different. Once you've done so much, there is still the fascination of the unknown. I am always drawn back to my early memory in 1969 when I was in Aradippou, walking with my *yiayia* (grandmother), going home on the night that the first men landed on the moon, and I wished I could also go into space. Well, it could become a reality after all! Wouldn't that be just great?

Acknowledgements

I am grateful to my family, who encouraged me to start this book, persevere with it and get it out into the world; in particular my daughter, Maria, whose idea it was for me to put down my story with the help of my amazing editor.

I would like to thank my editor Sophia Blackwell, who worked on the book with me, conducted and transcribed interviews, edited the manuscript and selected a publishing services company. She also put up with me for the last six years!

My thanks also go to my dear friends Egly Pantelakis and her brother Harris Hadjicharalambous, who read the book and provided very helpful comments.

Above all, I am grateful to my husband Philip, who worked hard with me to review each chapter in detail and provided his input and changes on the numerous versions of the book. I am thankful to him for his support and encouragement throughout my career and in our marriage.